AQA English and English Language

Foundation Tier

Revision Guide

GCSE

Imelda Pilgrim
Richard Broomhead

Nelson Thornes

Published in 2010 by:
Nelson Thornes Ltd
Delta Place
27 Bath Road
CHELTENHAM
GL53 7TH
United Kingdom

12 13 14 / 10 9 8 7 6 5 4 3

A catalogue record for this book is available from the British Library

ISBN 978 1 4085 0692 9

Illustrations by Harry Venning, Mark Draisey, Paul McCaffrey, Alan Rowe and
Seb Camagajevac

Cover photograph: Heather Gunn Photography

Page make-up by Pantek Arts Ltd, Maidstone

Printed in China

Acknowledgements
The authors and publishers wish to thank the following for permission to use
copyright material:

pp3, 8, 23, 26 and 29 (also pp4, 6, 7 (details)), www.mercattours.com; pp11
and 31 ©2010 Merlin Entertainments Group; pp13, 16, 23, 26 and 29 (also
p14 (detail) Scottish Natural Heritage; p18 Fotolia; pp21 and 31 Crown
copyright; pp33 and 36 (also pp38, 40, 55 and 57 (details)) WWF; p34
iStockphoto; pp43 and 60 WWF; pp45, 55 and 57 © BBC Worldwide Limited
(article), Getty Images (photos); p46 Getty Images; pp53 and 60 'Euroscarred'
12 February 2010, The Sun Online/nisyndication.com; pp63 and 66 'Haiti
earthquake' reproduced from emergencies web pages with the permission of
Save the Children UK. © 2010. All rights reserved; pp64, 68 and 70 'The day I
flew into HELL' 7 February 2010, Fabulous magazine/nisyndication.com; pp65
and 70 Unicef leaflet 'We promise will you' Unicef; p73 'A holiday that's out
of this world' based on article from www.travel-rants.com/2009/07/16/space-
tourism-takeoff (article). Rex Features (photo); p73 'Apollo 11: Where were
you when the Eagle landed?' 2 July 2009, The Guardian Online, copyright
Guardian News & Media Ltd 2009 (article). Corbis (photo); p74 Virgin
Galactic webpage, 'The Dream' www.virgingalactic.com/overview/experience,
Virgin Galactic; p84 iStockphoto; p89 iStockphoto; p90 Getty Images; p91
iStockphoto; p94 iStockphoto; p95 Getty Images; p99 Rex Features; p108
Heather Gunn Photography; p114 iStockphoto.

Every effort has been made to contact the copyright holders and we apologise
if any have been overlooked. Should copyright have been unwittingly infringed
in this book, the owners should contact the publishers, who will make
corrections at reprint.

Contents

Introduction to the book and exam.. iv

Section A — Reading

Reading introduction... 1

1 Exploring a web page.. 2
2 Examining an advert... 12
3 Making comparisons... 22
4 Exploring campaign material.. 32
5 Exploring a personal account... 44
6 More about comparison.. 54
7 Making your reading skills count in the exam................................. 61
8 Practice examination for the reading section................................. 72

Section B — Writing

Writing introduction... 75

9   Answering the question... 76
10 Communicating clearly.. 83
11 Sentence structures and vocabulary... 90
12 Technical accuracy... 96
13 Targeting your audience.. 103
14 Making your writing skills count in the exam................................. 109
15 Practice examination for the writing section................................. 116

Answers.. 117

AQA GCSE English and GCSE English Language

Nelson Thornes and AQA

Nelson Thornes has worked in partnership with AQA to ensure that the revision guide and the accompanying online resources offer you the best support possible for your GCSE exam. The print and online resources together **unlock blended learning**: this means that the links between the activities in the book and the activities online blend together to maximise your understanding of a topic and help you achieve your potential.

All AQA-endorsed products undergo a thorough quality assurance process to ensure that their contents closely match the AQA specification. You can be confident that the content of materials branded with AQA's 'Exclusively Endorsed' logo have been written, checked and approved by AQA senior examiners, in order to achieve AQA's exclusive endorsement.

About your exam

This book has been written to guide you through your GCSE English or GCSE English Language exam. It will remind you of the skills you need to succeed in your exams.

How to use this book

There are two sections of the book, covering Reading and Writing. You will be assessed on each of these skills by an exam. After you've worked through each section, you are shown how to use these skills effectively when being assessed in the 'Making your skills count' chapters. There is then a chapter with a practice exam for you to try. There are also reminders about how to punctuate and spell correctly. Remember, you will gain marks for being able to spell and punctuate your work accurately.

The features in this book include:

Objectives

At the beginning of each chapter you will find a list of learning objectives that contain targets linked to the requirements of the specification.

Activity

Activities to develop and reinforce the skills focus for the chapter.

Check your revision

What you should know and be able to do. Work through the questions to check what you've learned in the chapter.

Some (but not all) chapters feature:

Practice question

Use the skills that you've just learned to answer the questions. This will make sure you know and understand the points being made about how to apply your skills in the exam.

Top Tip

Guidance on how to avoid common pitfalls and mistakes, and how to achieve the best marks in the exam.

Key terms

Key term: a term that you will find useful to be able to define and understand. The definitions also appear in the glossary, which can be found in the free online resources (see below).

Online resources

Revision guide website

For FREE online resources, go to www.nelsonthornes.com/aqagcse/revision guides

kerboodle!

These online resources are available on *kerboodle!* which can be accessed via the internet at www.kerboodle.com/live, anytime, anywhere.

If your school or college subscribes to *kerboodle!* you will be provided with your own personal login details. Once logged in, access your course and locate the required activity.

Throughout the book you will see this icon whenever there is a relevant interactive activity available in *kerboodle!*

Please visit kerboodle.helpserve.com if you would like more information and help on how to use *kerboodle!*

Weblinks for this book

Because Nelson Thornes is not responsible for third party content online, there may be some changes to this material that are beyond our control. In order for us to ensure that the links referred to are as up-to-date and stable as possible, please let us know at webadmin@nelsonthornes.com if you find a link that doesn't work and we will do our best to redirect these, or to list an alternative site.

Introduction

About the exam

There is one exam paper in GCSE English and GCSE English Language. Its focus is **understanding and producing non-fiction texts**.

The paper is divided into two sections:

- **Section A**: Reading (one hour) and worth 20% of your final marks
- **Section B**: Writing (one hour) and worth 20% of your final marks.

In Section A, you will be asked to read three non-fiction items and answer five questions.

- Question 1 tests your ability to retrieve (find information).
- Question 2 assesses your skills of inference and reading between the lines (short question).
- Question 3 assesses your skills of inference and reading between the lines (longer question).
- Question 4 focuses on the language of one item you have read.
- Question 5 looks at comparison of the presentation of two items (of your choice).

The Assessment Objectives

To do well, you need to be clear about what skills are being tested.

The Assessment Objectives on which you will be tested are printed below. The annotations show you what they mean in terms of the skills you need to show your examiner.

Show skills such as inference, deduction, exploration and interpretation

Select and use material from two different texts in order to answer the final question

Read and understand texts, selecting material appropriate to purpose, collating from different sources and making comparisons and cross references as appropriate.

Select points from the items in order to answer the question

Point out similarities and differences between texts, and make connections between them

Comment on how effective features in a text are

Consider how the writer/designer is trying to manipulate the intended reader

Explain and evaluate how writers use linguistic, grammatical, structural and presentational features to achieve effects and influence the reader, supporting comments with detailed textual references.

Focus in detail on the techniques of the writers and designers

Examine and analyse the words and the order in which they are placed, the way the text is organised and the use of presentational features (the layout on the page)

Refer to the text in detail to support the points you make

Being prepared

When you take the exam you have one hour to complete the Reading section. The following chapters will help you to understand what is expected and ensure that you show the best of your reading skills in order to gain the most marks.

1

Objectives

In this chapter you will revise:

how to explore a web page

thinking about the ideas

how it has been organised

the use of language.

Key terms

Infer: show that you can interpret, explore meaning and deduce ideas.

Exploring a web page

Getting started

In your English or English Language examination you will be asked to explore the ideas in a text. This means show that you have understood what it is about and how this is presented to you.

Activity

1   Read Item 1.1, a web page for Mercat Tours, a company that provides activities and tours in Edinburgh and around the world.

List four different things that Mercat Tours advertises on their web page.

In order to complete Activity 1, you found relevant examples from the web page and wrote them down. You did not need to re-word these, just write them down in a list. This is an example of the first type of question that you may have to complete in the examination and it tests your literal understanding.

In further questions, you will need to show that you can **infer** meaning from words.

Activity

2   Now read the whole web page carefully. Make brief notes in answer to these questions:

a   On their web page Mercat Tours advertises more than eight things that it offers. What does this suggest about the company?

b   What do the words 'Engages, Enthrals & Entertains' suggest about what Mercat Tours offers?

c   What does the phrase saying that Mercat Tours 'provides the best' suggest about the company?

In Activity 2 you have just inferred meaning and made connections about what is being suggested by the company about itself. Now look at this question:

What does the writer of the web page suggest about Mercat Tours?

This question means you need to look at how the company makes itself sound to the reader.

Remember to refer to the details in the text to support your points.

Practice question

1 **a** Use your notes from Activities 1 and 2 to help you answer the question:

What does the writer of the web page suggest about Mercat Tours?

b Compare your answer with the sample one on page 4.

Item 1.1

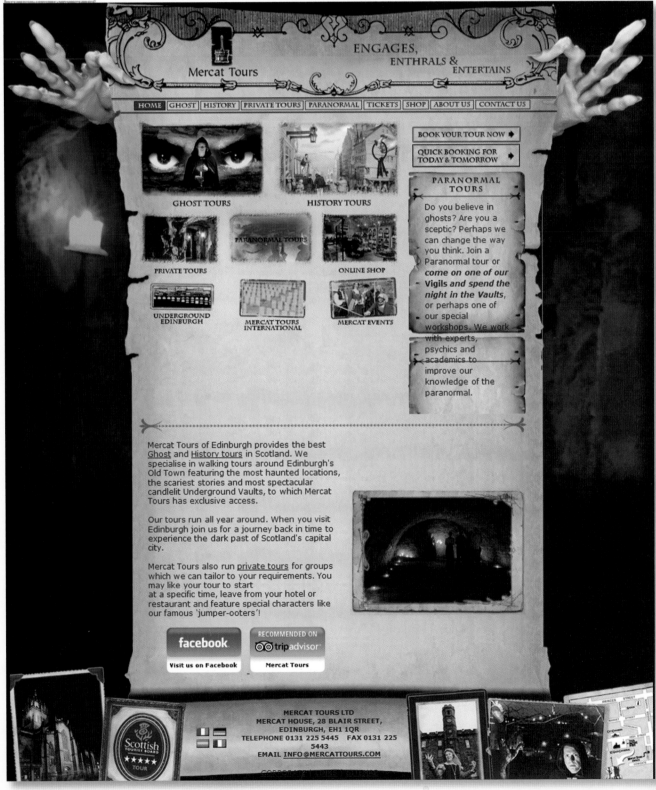

What does the writer of the web page suggest about Mercat Tours?

Mercat Tours lists several activities that it provides as a company and this suggests that it is trying to provide something for everyone from going on a ghost tour to shopping online. It uses words deliberately to suggest that it has exciting events shown by the words 'Engages, Enthrals and Entertains'. This means that people will be very interested and amused by what is on offer. This is also shown by the use of the phrase 'provides the best' giving the impression that no other company is as good as Mercat.

Referring to details in the text

In the examiner's mark scheme, it says that students need to 'offer relevant and appropriate quotation to support clear understanding'. This means that you must use examples from the text in your answer.

Activity

3　a　How many times does the student's answer to the Mercat Tours question give an example from the web page?

b　Now look at your own answer. How many times did you give an example from the text?

c　Place an asterisk (*) next to points where you think you could have given an example from the web page but did not.

In the sample answer that you have read, the examples from the web page are included within the answer. They are used to support the points made by the student.

Top Tip

To achieve Grade C at Foundation, always include examples from the text to support your points.

Understanding structure and presentation

Structure means how a text (images and writing) is organised and set out on the page. Presentation is when you look at the various presentational features that are used. These include features such as:

● colour

● fonts

● illustrations.

In the examination, you might be asked to write about specific features (such as the use of illustrations) or to write more generally about how structure and presentation are used. You need to be ready for either type of question.

Activity

4 Make notes on the following questions about the presentation and structure of the Mercat Tours web page:

a What do you think is the most striking aspect of the web page?

b Which part of the web page catches your eye the most? Can you give a reason for this?

c Which part of the web page do you think is the least eye-catching? Suggest a reason for this.

Now look at this spidergram, which shows a student's ideas on different presentational features:

This student has shown the ability to select the correct type of presentational features. However, this is just like a list. To gain higher grades, the student needs to use their skills of inference and interpretation to suggest *why* the features are used. They need to think about why the designer of the web page has used the features.

Sample question and answer

Look at the following extract from a student's answer. The highlighted parts show where the student is using skills of inference and interpretation.

How is the background presented to interest the reader?

The background is a scroll to make it look old fashioned and something ancient from the past. The scroll is held by a skeleton's bony hands suggesting that what you will see might be unexpected and frightening. The scroll also suggests that Mercat Tours provides activities that take you back in time and teach you more about history from a long time ago as it is also ripped and torn.

2 You are now going to try answering this question on your own:

> How have images been used in the web page to interest the reader?

Use these prompts to help you:

- Looking back at the spidergram and using ideas of your own, write a paragraph about the *images*.
- Highlight the parts of your answer that show where you have used inference and interpretation.

Exploring language

In Practice 2 and Activity 4, you showed that you can look closely at how a text is presented and come up with your own interpretations. You also need to show the examiner that you can explore and comment on the use of language. This chart shows what you need to include in your answer to gain a particular grade.

Top Tip

Using words such as 'suggests', 'shows' and 'implies' will help you to interpret and make inferences.

Language technique	Example from web page	Comment on why it is used
Grade E		
Grade D		
Grade C		

Read the following extract from a student's answer. They are answering the question:

> How are **superlatives** used for effect on the web page?

Key terms

Superlatives: words or phrases that show that something is better than another thing – it is of the highest quality. Look out for words such as 'greatest; 'largest'; 'most'.

In the first paragraph several superlatives are deliberately used. One example is the word 'best' that suggests that no other tour company can beat this company and this might persuade people to book with them. Also, the word 'scariest' shows that the company puts a lot of effort into making their tours very good as people often enjoy being frightened. Finally, 'most spectacular' makes their events sound amazing and much better than anyone else's as 'most' suggests that Mercat Tours is the best.

The highlighted parts show where the student has explored and commented on the use of language.

Activity

5 Copy the following table.

- Column one lists language techniques that are used in the web page.
- Column two is for an example from the web page.
- Column three is where you interpret and infer why the language technique is used.

Language technique	Example from web page	Comment on why it is used
Questions	Do you believe in ghosts?	Involves the reader, draws them into the text and suggests what the rest of the writing will be about
Addresses reader directly	When **you** visit Edinburgh	
Directives	Join a paranormal tour …	
Pattern of three ideas	Engages, enthrals & entertains	

Complete column three. Then highlight the parts of your comment that show where you have inferred or interpreted.

There are other language techniques that you might have noticed when reading, such as alliteration ('Engages, Enthrals and Entertains') or short sentences ('Our tours run all year around'). In order to move towards gaining Grade C you need to make sure that you focus mainly on the quality of your comment (column three in the table). It is not just a case of spotting language techniques and giving examples, it is about explaining why the writer has used them. In the examination, try to pick about three language techniques, give an example and then comment on why the writer has used them.

Evaluating effectiveness

You may be asked to evaluate the effectiveness of the presentation and/or language of a text.

In order to evaluate the effectiveness of a text, you have to work out its intended audience and purpose. Remember, a text might have more than one audience and purpose. For example, a television advert for a product might be aiming to inform and persuade (**purpose**) and be targeting children and teenagers (**audience**).

Top Tip

If you are asked in the exam to 'evaluate effectiveness', this means to consider how successful the language and/or presentation is by giving your own opinion.

Key terms

Purpose: the reason that a text is written (to argue, advise, etc.).

Audience: who the text is written for or aimed at (pensioners, men, etc.).

6 **a** Which of the following purposes is appropriate to the web page? Copy and complete the table.

Possible purpose	Reasons why you think this might be a purpose
To inform the reader about Mercat Tours	
To persuade the reader to book a tour with the company	
To frighten people and put them off Edinburgh	
To explain the history of Edinburgh	

i Which purpose do you think is the most appropriate?

ii Which purpose do you think is the least appropriate?

b Which of the following audiences is the web page aimed at? Copy and complete the table.

Possible audience	Reasons why you think this might be a possible audience
Visitors to Scotland	
Children under the age of five	
People who do not believe in ghosts	
People who want a tour that is unique for them	

i Which audience(s) do you think the web page is the *most* likely to appeal to?

ii Which audience(s) do you think the web page is *least* likely to appeal to?

In any answer in which you evaluate a text, you need to show the examiner that you have thought about:

- how well it achieves its intended purpose(s)
- how well it reaches its intended audience(s).

Look at the following question, which focuses on the use of language.

How does the writer use language to make the web page <u>exciting</u> and <u>persuade</u> the reader to book a tour?

Read the following, which is part of a student's answer to this question. The student has focused on the 'exciting' part of the question. The annotations show where the student is fulfilling the examiner's mark scheme and therefore doing the right thing!

Exciting

The first example of language that makes the web page seem exciting is the use of alliteration and a pattern of three ideas✓ 'Engages, Enthrals and Entertains'✓. Each word begins with the letter 'E' to make it stick in the reader's mind but also each word makes the tour sound great as 'engages' makes it seem like✓ you'll be really hooked, 'enthrals' suggests you will be totally amazed on the tour and 'entertains' indicates that it will be fun.✓ The writer also uses humour to make the web page sound exciting when it says 'you may like your tour ... to feature special characters like our famous "jumper-ooters"!' The humour here is 'jumper-ooters' as it suggests that people will frighten✓ and scare you on your tour by jumping out on you but 'ooters' is also a joke on the Scottish accent as it is set in Edinburgh.

Recognises language techniques

Comments on effects of language

Uses appropriate quotation to support point

Shows inference and interpretation

Some focus on purpose

Notice how the student has drawn together the skills from the whole of this unit in order to produce a good and detailed answer.

Practice question

3 **a** Now try to answer the 'persuade' part of the question. Use the model you have just read to explore how the writer tries to persuade the reader to book a tour. Remember to:

   i show you can recognise language techniques

   ii give examples from the web page to support your ideas

   iii comment on how language is used by inferring and interpreting.

   b Once you have completed your answer, look at it and highlight where you have achieved each of the three points listed above. Then have a look at the student's attempt at the second part of the question. How similar is it to yours? Have you missed anything that the student below achieved?

Persuade

As well as using language to excite the reader, it is also used to persuade. The writer uses a directive✓ to try to persuade the reader to decide what Mercat Tours is like for themselves, 'Join one of our Vigils'.✓ This is trying to make the reader try the company out✓ without too much pressure.✓ Also, the writer deliberately uses the verb 'specialise'✓ to imply that the company is able to provide unique tours that are different from normal.✓ This makes the company sound like no other✓ and is able to suit everyone's needs.✓

Shows inference

Comment on effects of language

Comment on effects of language

Some focus on audience

Recognises language technique

Uses appropriate quotation to support point

Aware of writer's purpose and recognises language technique

Shows inference

Check your revision

You are now going to find out how well you have understood this chapter. Opposite (in Item 1.2) you will see another web page that is similar to the one you have explored in detail. It is about entertainment at Warwick Castle, a visitor attraction.

Read Item 1.2 and complete the activities below. Use the bullet points to help you.

Reading with understanding

List four things that you can do at Warwick Castle.

- Remember that this question tests your literal understanding, so you just need to find four examples and write them down.

Commenting on structure and presentation

Write a short paragraph about the main photograph on the web page.

- Why has it been used?
- What does it suggest about what you can experience at Warwick Castle?

Remember that you need to:

- show that you can infer and interpret
- refer to details in the picture to support your comments.

Thinking about language

How has the writer of the web page used language to persuade the reader to visit Warwick Castle? Use the following extract from the web page to write your answer.

> **Imagine a totally electrifying, full day out at Britain's Ultimate Castle.**
>
> Where you can immerse yourself in a thousand years of jaw-dropping history – come rain or shine. Where ancient myths and spell-binding tales will set your imagination alight and your hair on end. Where princesses are pampered and maidens are wooed.

Remember that you need to:

- find examples of language techniques
- give specific examples from the text
- comment on how the language has been used to persuade the reader.

Evaluating effectiveness

How has the web page been presented to make it effective?

Remember to:

- work out the intended audience(s) and purpose(s)
- compose your own comments on how effective the page is
- support your ideas with examples from the text
- show that you can infer and interpret
- include any extra ideas of your own.

Assessment

Use this checklist:

- Reread your answers.
- Highlight in one colour the comments you have made that show inference and interpretation.
- Use another colour to highlight where you have used examples from the text (quotations).
- Use a third colour if you have made any extra comments of your own.

HOME   TICKETS & OFFERS   **ENTERTAINMENT**   PLAN YOUR DAY   SCHOOLS   GROUPS   EVENTS

Switch to low graphics version

Wednesday 26th May 2010

EVENTS
REINVENTED >>

EXCLUSIVE OFFERS!

Save up to 20%

Tickets

BUY TICKETS ONLINE

Events Calendar: 2010

Imagine a totally electrifying, full day out at Britain's Ultimate Castle.

Where you can immerse yourself in a thousand years of jaw-dropping history – come rain or shine. Where ancient myths and spell-binding tales will set your imagination alight and your hair on end. Where princesses are pampered and maidens are wooed.

Experience the heat of battle at such close quarters you'll almost smell the fear, as winners become true heroes and losers are confined to dark, dank dungeons to be forgotten for eternity.

It could only be Warwick Castle.

FIND IT FAST!

Ticket prices   >>
Opening times   >>
How to get here   >>
Register for offers   >>
Tell a friend   >>

| **May** | June | July | August | September | October | November |

May

Jousting Returns for Whitsun Half Term

29th May – 6th June

Jousting Returns With a Barbaric Twist This Whit Week at Warwick Castle

For all those looking to step back in time this Whit week, Warwick Castle is inviting you to saddle up and ride over to Britain's Ultimate Castle to experience an adventure for all the family to enjoy.

The famous **Jousting Knights** return to the Castle grounds from **29 May**, but this time, they are not alone. The rebel Barbarians are planning to invade the Castle and challenge the valiant Warwick warriors to the ultimate fight.

The bravery, skill and agility of the jousters will be tested to the fullest, guaranteeing the crowds a dazzling show as their incredible equestrian prowess and pageantry on the field is displayed.

All budding explorers set to conquer the Castle will be able take part in **A Knight's Quest** a discovery trail like no other. Those brave enough will uncover runes and clues from all over the grounds even climbing the mound – the oldest part of the Castle grounds built in 1068. Can you complete the trail and recover the long lost treasure?

Visitors to the Castle will be able to admire the magnificent mediaeval weaponry collection. Witness the **Trebuchet**, fired twice daily and the replica **Ballista** as historical battles are brought back to life with these deadly military machines – noted to be the most dangerous of all time.

If that's not enough to keep you and the kids busy, every day throughout the holidays, visitors can catch the mediaeval bowman's awe-inspiring **archery display**, watch the return of Nikita the sea eagle in the Castle's stunning **Flight of the Eagles show** and meet the resident **falconer** and his birds of prey.

To top it all off, the Castle Dungeon, will be open and receiving victims. The attraction recreates some of the darkest chapters in the Castle's history, from the terrors of the torture chamber to the foul pestilence of the plague.

12 months entry to top UK attractions - find out more!

Experience more. Take the Warwick Castle Virtual Tour.

Objectives

In this chapter you will revise:

how to explore an advert

thinking about the ideas

how it is organised

the ways language is used.

Examining an advert

Getting started

In your English or English Language examination you will be asked to look at the ideas in a text. That means show that you have understood what it is about and how this is revealed to you.

In order to complete Activity 1, you need to find and write down four examples from the advert. Remember to look carefully at the *trigger* word in the question. Here it is 'list', meaning just write it down as a list. There may be more than four examples that you can give, but stick to the number asked for in the question.

Activity

1. Read the advert, which gives advice to people who are camping in Scotland.

   List four pieces of advice the advert gives people in order that they can be responsible campers.

The next type of question in the examination focuses on your ability to infer or read between the lines. This means that you look at what is *suggested* but not said directly.

Activity

2. Read the following quotation from Item 2.1:

   'Hey big man. If you're careless with fire, I'll splat on your tent!'

   Make brief notes in answer to these questions:

   a   Why has a talking bird been used in the advert?

   b   Why does the bird refer to the reader as 'big man'?

   c   Why does the bird threaten to 'splat on your tent'?

In your answers to the questions in Activity 2, you have inferred meaning and made connections about what is being suggested. Now look at this question:

How effective is using a talking bird in the advert?

Practice question

1. a   Use your notes and ideas from Activities 1 and 2 to help you answer the question:

      How effective is using a talking bird in the advert?

   b   Compare your answer with the one on page 14.

Item 2.1

DON'T MESS WITH NATURE

Hey big man. If you're careless with fire, I'll *splat* on your tent!

If you're camping with your mates this summer don't mess with nature. Here's a few pointers for you to follow ....or else!

HOW TO CAMP RESPONSIBLY:

LIGHTING FIRES. Never cut down or damage trees. Use a stove if possible. If you must have an open fire keep it small and under control and remove all traces before leaving.

HUMAN WASTE. Carry a trowel and bury your own waste and urinate well away from open water, rivers and burns.

LITTER. Take away all your rubbish and consider picking up other litter as well.

PARKING. Use a designated car park where possible and never block a road or lane, an entrance to a field or a building.

KNOW THE CODE BEFORE YOU GO
outdooraccess-scotland.com
SCOTTISH OUTDOOR ACCESS CODE

How effective is using a talking bird in the advert?

The designer of the advert has used a talking bird for effect. Because it is aimed at younger people, a cartoon bird that talks is more likely to appeal to this age group since they will have watched cartoons as younger children. The bird's first word 'hey' is informal and casual to attract the target audience and 'big man' is cleverly used to show that the people who use the countryside for camping are bigger than the wildlife that lives there and so the creatures are more vulnerable to the mess that people create. The writer uses humour in the words 'splat on your tent' because the bird will make its own mess to add to the mess created by campers.

Focuses on target audience

Shows inference and deduction

Effects of language

Shows inference and deduction

Shows inference and deduction

The highlighted text in the answer shows where the student is able to infer and read between the lines. By showing the examiner that you can do this, you have a better chance of achieving Grade C.

Referring to details in the text

In the examiner's mark scheme, it says that students need to 'offer relevant and appropriate quotation to support clear understanding'. This means that you have to use examples from the text in your answer.

Activity

3

a How many times does the student's answer to the question about the talking bird give an example from the advert?

b Now look at your own answer. How many times did you give an example from the advert?

c Place an asterisk (*) next to points where you think you could have given an example from the advert but did not.

In the sample answer that you have read, the examples from the advert are included within the answer. They are used to support the points made by the student.

Top Tip

To reach Grade C at Foundation, always include examples from the text to support your points.

Understanding structure and presentation

You looked at structure and presentation in Chapter 1. Structure means how a text (images and writing) is organised and presented on the page. Presentation is when you look at the various presentational features that are used. These include features such as:

- colour
- headings
- cartoons and images.

In the examination, you might be asked to write about specific features (such as the use of headings) or to write more generally about how structure and presentation are used. You need to be prepared for either type of question.

Activity

4   Look at the whole advert in Item 2.1 and see how it is presented. Copy and complete the table below which focuses on the presentation and structure of the leaflet.

Focus on presentation and structure	Your ideas
Why do you think a cartoon has been used in the leaflet?	
Why is the word 'splat' presented in this way?	
Why is the language of the headings slang or informal?	
Why is the text presented in short paragraphs?	
Why do you think the heading is presented in capital letters?	

Now focus on this question:

How have two different presentational devices been used to interest the reader?

Look at this spidergram, which shows a student's ideas about two different presentational features.

easy to follow and understand

support writing/ text

Cartoons

suit audience of young people

try to add a little humour and make ideas less worrying

font suggests that the splat will go everywhere as it has splashes on it

Splat

adds humour to the advert

presented in white to stand out

matches the colour of bird excrement

The student's spidergram shows some good ideas about why a cartoon is used as a presentational feature in the advert. This is a good starting point. However, to gain higher grades, the student needs to use their skills of inference and interpretation to suggest why the designer of the advert has used the features. Look at the student's written answer. The highlighted parts show where the student infers and interprets why cartoons are used.

> A cartoon is used in the advert as a presentational feature. This adds to the text by presenting the same information in a more visual way to make sure that the reader has understood the key point. Younger people tend to prefer visual information and using a cartoon means that there is less to read. The presentation of the word 'splat' is in white to reflect the colour of bird excrement and the font has splashes to suggest that it will make a mess. This adds humour as the bird is gently pointing out that it wants its habitat and the Scottish countryside kept tidy. Added to this, the way in which the bird is standing with its wing on its hip makes it seem like it is making a threat. Obviously, the bird cannot do much damage to a camper so this increases the humour.

Practice question

2. **a** Look back at the spidergram. Use it together with your own ideas and write a paragraph about the *heading*. Use the example answer above to help you develop your comments.

   b Highlight the parts of your answer that show where you have used inference and interpretation. Look for other places where you might have written 'suggests' or 'shows'.

Exploring language

In the examination you will also need to consider how writers use language for effect. Look at how the following student writes about how the author talks directly to the reader. The highlighted parts show where the student has used skills of inference and interpretation.

The writer of the advert talks directly to the reader using the pronoun 'you' which makes it seem more personal and like a conversation. For example: 'If you're camping' and 'Here's a few pointers for you to follow'. This involves the reader as it makes it feel like the bird is singling them out to give advice about camping in Scotland and to stress the importance of keeping the countryside clean.

Activity

5   a   Copy and complete the table below. Column one lists language techniques that are used in the advert. Column two is for a quotation from the advert. Column three is where you interpret and infer why the language technique is used.

Language technique	Example from advert	Comment on why it is used
Directives	Take away all your rubbish	
Use of slang/ informal language	camping with your mates	
Subject-specific words	damage, traces, waste	

  b   In column three, highlight any text where you show that you have inferred or interpreted.

It is important to know what sort of language techniques are used (column one) and to give examples to support your ideas (column two). However, the most important part of an answer is the quality of your comment on why a technique is used (column three). This is the part that gains you most marks. So, in the examination, try to pick about three language techniques, give an example and then comment on why and how the writer has used each one.

Evaluating effectiveness

In the exam, you may be asked to evaluate the effectiveness of the presentation and/or the language of a text.

To do this, you have to work out its intended audience and purpose. Remember that a text might have more than one audience and purpose.

6 **a** Which of the following purposes is appropriate to the advert? Copy and complete the table.

Possible purpose	Reasons why you think this might be a purpose
To advise the reader about camping in Scotland	
To persuade young people to be responsible when camping	
To warn young people about what could happen to them if they are irresponsible campers	
To explain how to look after the Scottish countryside	

   i Which purpose do you think is the most appropriate?

   ii Which purpose do you think is the least appropriate?

b Which of the following audiences is the advert aimed at? Copy and complete the table.

Possible audience	Reasons why you think this might be a possible audience
The general public who go camping	
Young people who go camping	
Older people who go camping	

   i Which audience(s) do you think the advert is most likely to be aimed at?

   ii Which audience(s) do you think the advert is least likely to be aimed at?

In any answer in which you evaluate a text, you need to show the examiner that you have thought about:

- how well it achieves its intended purpose(s)
- how well it reaches its intended audience(s).

Look at the following question and answer, which focuses on the use of language.

> How is language used to suit the intended audience of the advert? Comment on:
>
> - the use of informal language
> - the use of **directives**.

Read part of the student's answer to this question. They have focused on 'the use of informal language' part of the question. The annotations show where the student is fulfilling the examiner's mark scheme and therefore doing the right thing!

Key terms

Directives: words that give orders, commands or advice. Look out for them at the start of sentences such as 'Turn over to answer question 6'. 'Turn over' is the directive.

Recognises language techniques

The use of informal language
Because the leaflet is aimed at young people, the writer has used language deliberately to suit them and encourage them to read it. For example, the writer uses slang to appeal to his audience: 'If you're camping with your mates ...'. Here the word 'mates' is used to appeal to the younger audience instead of the word 'friends' – this makes it more informal and more suited to a younger reader. This means that the intended audience is more likely to engage with the advert's ideas. Similarly, 'hey big man' is used to appeal more to a younger reader as it is casual and relaxed. The word 'splat' is deliberately used to add humour and suggest what the bird might do to those who break the simple rules.

Uses appropriate quotation to support point

Comments on effects of language

Recognises language techniques

Shows inference and interpretation

Notice how the student has drawn together the skills from the whole of this unit in order to produce a good and detailed answer.

Practice question

3 **a** Now try to answer 'the use of directives' part of the question. Use the model you have just read to explore how the writer tries to reach his intended audience.

   i Show that you can recognise language techniques.

   ii Give examples from the advert to support your ideas.

   iii Comment on how language is used by inferring and interpreting.

   b Once you have completed your answer, have a look at the student's attempt at the second part of the question.

   i How similar is it to yours?

   ii Which parts of the examiner's mark scheme are you confident that you achieve?

Recognises language techniques

Uses appropriate quotation to support point

Comments on effects of language

Comments on effects of language

The use of directives
The writer uses directives to give advice to the reader in order to keep the Scottish countryside tidy. The first directive appears in the heading 'Don't mess with nature'. The reader is told directly and very clearly to avoid ruining the countryside. Most of the directives are used at the bottom of the advert to reinforce keeping things tidy. For example, 'Carry a trowel and bury ...' gives advice and suggestions in a non-threatening way meaning that hopefully the reader will act upon the advice.

Shows inference and interpretation

Shows inference and interpretation

Check your revision

You are now going to find out how well you have understood this chapter. Read Item 2.2, a leaflet called 'How much will your next round cost you?' and complete the activities below using the bullet points to help you.

Reading with understanding

List four things that could happen to someone who is caught drink-driving.

Remember that this question tests your literal understanding, so you just need to find four examples and write them down.

Commenting on structure and presentation

Write a short paragraph on the main images used in the leaflet.

- Why is the background blurred?
- Why are the four bottles used?

Remember that you need to:

- show that you can infer and interpret
- refer to details in the pictures to support your comments.

Thinking about language

How has the writer of the leaflet used language to make the reader think about drinking and driving? Use the following extract from the leaflet to write your answer.

'So imagine for a moment relying on your friends and family to drive you wherever you need to go:

- Planning even the most basic trip to the cinema or shops around the local bus or train schedule.
- Having to sell your car to pay a hefty fine or just watching it rust away for 12 months.

Now picture yourself having to find a new job. Because without a licence you can't drive to work or drive for work:

- Plenty of employers refuse to hire people with criminal records.
- How will it feel explaining the story of your criminal record at every job interview you go to?'

Remember that you need to:

- find examples of language techniques
- give specific examples from the text
- comment on how the language has been used to persuade the reader.

Evaluating effectiveness

How has the leaflet been presented to make it effective?

Remember to:

- work out the intended audience(s) and purpose(s)
- make your own comments on how effective the leaflet is
- support your ideas with examples from the text
- show that you can infer and interpret
- include any extra ideas of your own.

Assessment

Use this checklist:

- Reread your answers.
- Highlight in one colour any comments you have made that show inference and interpretation.
- Use another colour to highlight where you have used examples from the text (quotations).
- Use a third colour if you have made any extra comments of your own.

Item 2.2

What drink driving could cost you

- A court conviction
- A driving ban of at least 12 months
- An endorsement of your driving licence for 11 years
- A criminal record

If you get caught drink driving the consequences listed above are the minimum that will happen to you. You may also be liable to a fine of up to £5,000 and up to 6 months in prison.

But nothing on that list reflects the everyday consequences of being caught drink driving.

To understand that, you'll have to use your imagination.

So imagine for a moment relying on your friends and family to drive you wherever you need to go:

- Planning even the most basic trip to the cinema or shops around the local bus or train schedule
- Having to sell your car to pay a hefty fine or just watching it rust away for 12 months

Now picture yourself having to find a new job. Because without a licence you can't drive to work, or drive for work:

- Plenty of employers refuse to hire people with criminal records
- How will it feel explaining the story of your criminal record at every job interview you go to?

It won't happen to me

Last year, around 100,000 drivers across the country thought they could get away with drink driving.

If you think you won't get caught, you're wrong. The police are trained to spot all the tricks drink drivers use to avoid being caught:

- They can ask you to take a breath test just for suspecting you've been drinking or if you commit a traffic offence whilst driving
- You don't need to be involved in a crash

There's always an alternative

Most drink drivers don't plan to break the law. So to make sure you don't become another statistic, here are several ways you can avoid drinking and driving:

- Book a taxi. To make sure you get one, book it as early as you can in the evening
- At the start of the night agree who's driving and not drinking
- Use public transport routes to help you get home
- If you're at a friend's house, stay overnight
- Don't get into a car driven by someone else who's been drinking

And the morning after…

Don't rush to get behind the wheel the morning after you've been out drinking. You may feel fine but you could still be over the legal alcohol limit* or unfit to drive.

A cold shower, a cup of coffee or any of the other myths about 'sobering up' won't make you fit to drive any quicker. It just takes time to get the alcohol out of your system.

*The legal alcohol limit for driving in the UK is 80 milligrammes of alcohol in 100 millilitres of blood

CRIMINAL RECORD

£5000 Fine

YOUR JOB

12 Month Driving Ban

3

Objectives

In this chapter you will revise:

selecting and using material from different texts

looking at similarities and differences between two texts

making relevant comments on them

writing a comparison.

Making comparisons

In your English or English Language examination, one of the reading questions will ask you to compare two texts. You will be given a specific focus for the question. This might be looking at similarities and differences in language, audience, purpose or the presentation and organisation of the texts.

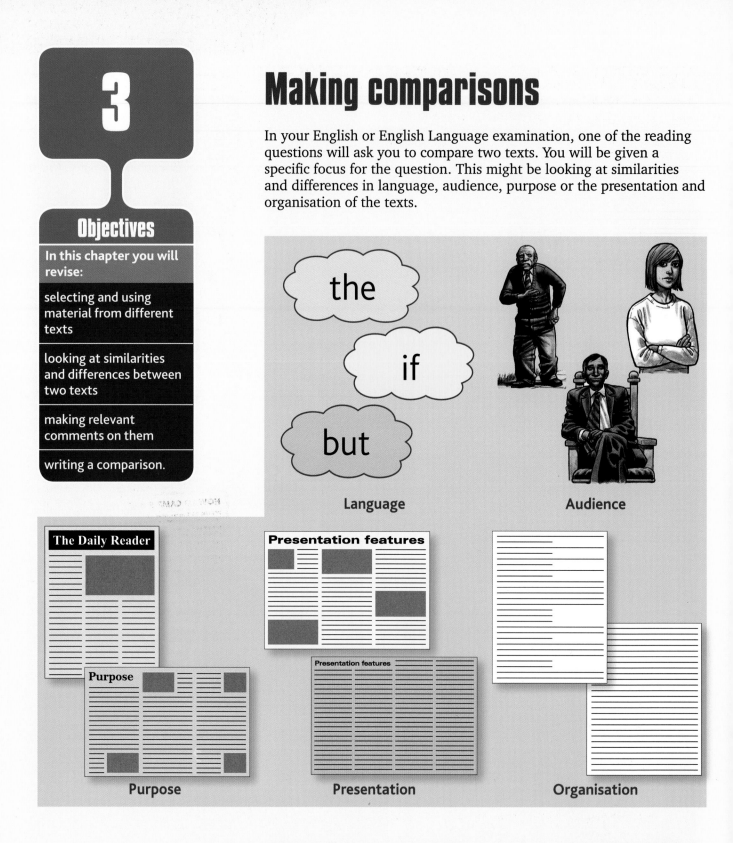

Language

Audience

Purpose

Presentation

Organisation

Look again at Item 1.1 (page 3), a web page advertising supernatural events, and Item 2.1 (page 13), an advert about camping responsibly. Remind yourself of the work that you have already done on these.

Looking at both texts generally on the page, think about any similarities and differences between the Items. These may be to do with language, audience, purpose, presentation and/or organisation. Record your ideas in a table like the one below. A few ideas have been added to get you started.

Item 1.1: Mercat Tours – web page	Item 2.1: 'Hey big man' – advert
Uses colour – black, brown, beige	Uses colour – turquoise, white, black
Uses images – old and new ones	Uses cartoon
General audience	Younger audience

Now that you have a list of ideas, you are going to look at how to start comparing those ideas.

The skills you need to show

Many students find the final question in the English/English Language examination the most demanding. This might be because you are asked to compare two of the three texts that you have read. One way of making sure that you definitely compare is to use words and phrases that will help you to make comparisons.

Words that show similarities	Words that show differences
Similarly	However
Also	On the other hand
Equally	In contrast with
In the same way as	Alternatively
As well as	But

You can probably think of other words that could also be used. Using these words and phrases in your answer, with a good choice of techniques, examples and comments, will help you to do well.

Look at how these words are included in an answer to signal that the writer is able to compare. The highlighted words trigger where the student is comparing.

> Both Items are presented in colour to interest the audience and as this is often expected today. Item 1.1 uses faded and old fashioned colours to suggest the past, but Item 2.1 is bright and bold as this will appeal to younger readers. Similarly, they both contain pictures to add variety and detail to the text. However, Item 2.1 uses a picture that is a cartoon and more suited to a younger audience whereas Item 1.1 includes old and modern photographs to suggest that the company caters for all tastes, ages and interests.

Add three more sentences based on ideas in your table, and continue comparing both Items. Make sure that you use key words that show you are comparing – look back at the table.

Comparing presentation and organisation

In the examination, you may be asked to compare some aspect of the presentation of two texts. In Activity 1 you are going to focus on the use of pictures in Items 1.1 and 2.1.

Top Tip

Students who make a quick plan of a question that asks them to compare often gain a better mark. This is because they have thought about it before writing!

Look at how a student has identified the key words of the following question.

> Look at similarities and differences

> The ways in which

Compare how pictures are used in both Items.

> The images – notice that there is just one focus for this task

Now look at the student's evidence and notes based on Items 1.1 and 2.1.

Presentation	Item 1.1	Effect	Item 2.1	Effect
Picture(s)	Various – pumpkin, old-fashioned images, ghostly images	Links to subject – variety of images to suggest wide range of events provided by company – images match text	Cartoon – an aggressive-looking bird advising young people to look after the countryside when camping	Suits younger reader – makes subject easier to follow – adds light humour to text

Here the student uses their notes to structure an answer to the question.

Now read the student's answer and the examiner's comments.

Key word to show comparison →

Pictures are used in both Items to make them more interesting and appealing to the reader. Item 1.1 contains several images connected with the topic of the web page which is the supernatural. Pictures such as a pumpkin, old-fashioned shots or ghostly images are used to support the text. Because several pictures are shown, this suggests that the company provides a range of events to suit all tastes. However, in Item 2.1, a cartoon is used to suit an audience of younger people. This shows an aggressive-looking bird advising young people to look after the countryside when camping. The cartoon is effective because it makes the subject easier to follow and sums up what is said in words in just a picture. It is also meant to bring some humour to what could otherwise be a boring topic for a teenager – as the advert is to make them more aware about the environment when camping.

Infers and interprets
Considers effects
Focus on audience

Considers effects

← Infers and interprets
← Key word to show comparison

← Considers effects

Examiner comment: The student approaches this question well. The student:

- uses supporting examples of presentation from each Item
- compares by making the point that both Items use pictures for similar reasons
- considers and explores possible effects
- infers and interprets.

Top Tip

When approaching an examination question, try to:

- highlight the key words in the question
- spend a few minutes gathering evidence and making notes
- write your answer using your notes and looking back at the key words in the question.

Practice question

1   Compare how colour is used in both Items.

    a   Highlight and annotate the key words in this question.

    b   Copy and complete the table below with evidence and ideas.

Presentation	Item 1.1	Effect	Item 2.1	Effect

    c   Write a paragraph answering the question.

    d   Highlight where you have shown that you can:

       i   compare

       ii   consider effects

       iii   infer and interpret

       iv   refer to audience and/or purpose

       v   use supporting examples.

Comparing audience

You have already looked at the audiences of both Items in Chapters 1 and 2. The audience of a text is the person or people that it is aimed at or written for. You can often work out the intended audience by looking at the features of the presentation.

Activity

1   Look back at Items 1.1 and 2.1 and then copy and complete the table below by ticking the relevant audiences for each Item.

Possible audience	Item 1.1 – web page	Item 2.1 – advert
Young children		
Teenagers		
Parents		
General public		
Retired people		
People who are interested in ghosts		
People who are interested in the countryside		

2 Look at how a student tackled Activity 1. What features of presentation can you find to support your decisions about the audiences of each Item?

Look at the student's notes.

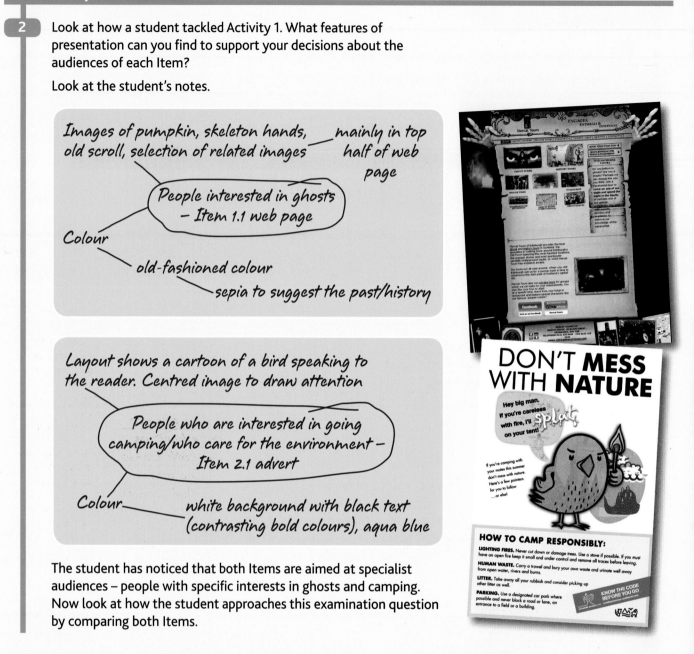

Images of pumpkin, skeleton hands, old scroll, selection of related images — mainly in top half of web page

People interested in ghosts – Item 1.1 web page

Colour

old-fashioned colour

sepia to suggest the past/history

Layout shows a cartoon of a bird speaking to the reader. Centred image to draw attention

People who are interested in going camping/who care for the environment – Item 2.1 advert

Colour — white background with black text (contrasting bold colours), aqua blue

The student has noticed that both Items are aimed at specialist audiences – people with specific interests in ghosts and camping. Now look at how the student approaches this examination question by comparing both Items.

Look at similarities and differences

Focus on techniques that are used

The ways the Items are set out

Whom the Items are written for

Compare how two Items use presentation to suit their audience.

Compare them using these headings:

- the use of images
- the layout of the Items.

Remember that whatever the question focuses on, you will be asked to write about the techniques that are used. In this question, the word 'how' is directing you to look at the techniques of presentation. At other times, the question might say:

- The methods …
- The ways …
- How does …

and each of these is asking you to write about the techniques.

This is the student's answer.

Makes comparison	Both Items (the web page and the advert) are aimed at specialist audiences as Item 1.1 is aimed at people with an interest in the paranormal and Item 2.1 is aimed at younger people who may be planning to go camping in the countryside. The web page places images mainly at the top and bottom as this is where we would begin reading and scroll down to the end so that they stick in our mind and support the text. However, the advert uses one image and places it centrally as the reader will see the whole page at once and often our eyes are drawn to the centre where we tend to expect images to be placed. Equally, both Items are presented to suit their target audience. The web page is made to look old with a scroll and faded colours to suggest the past and the advert contains a cartoon (to suit younger people) that is connected with the countryside (a bird). Both use presentation to suit their target audience but the advert is more focused on its audience as it uses a cartoon which older people might not like and the language is more informal and relaxed than the web page.

Annotations (left): Makes comparison · Infers and interprets · Infers and interprets · Key word to show comparison · Key word to show comparison · Key word to show comparison · Makes comparison

Annotations (right): Selects relevant examples to support point · Key word to show comparison · Selects relevant examples to support point · Infers and interprets · Infers and interprets · Key word to show comparison

Examiner comment: The student answers this question well.

The student:

- covers 'the use of images' and 'the layout of the Items' as per the question
- refers to the presentation
- compares by making the point that both Items are aimed at specialist audiences
- shows evidence of having inferred and deduced.

2 Read these two short advertisements.

Compare the ways in which these adverts use presentation to suit their audiences.

Comment on:
- the use of images
- the way each advertisement is presented.

Before you attempt the question:
- highlight the words that are key to answering the question correctly
- gather your evidence and ideas.

Write your answer.

Once you have written your answer, highlight to check that you have:
- focused on the use of images
- referred to how each advert is presented
- compared
- inferred and interpreted.

Purpose

The purpose of a text is the reason why it has been written. A text might have one main purpose as well as several other ones. For example, a persuasive advert's *main* purpose would be to persuade, but at the same time it might be to inform and advise the reader. You can find clues about purpose in the words that are used as well as in the presentation.

Activity

3

Compare the purposes of the two Items.

a   Highlight and annotate the key words in the question.

b   Look again at Items 1.1 and 2.1. Then copy and complete the table below by ticking the relevant purposes for each Item.

Purpose	Item 1.1 – web page	Item 2.1 – advert
To argue		
To advise		
To inform		
To persuade		
To narrate		
To analyse		

Now look at a student's spidergrams containing their ideas on the purposes of both Items.

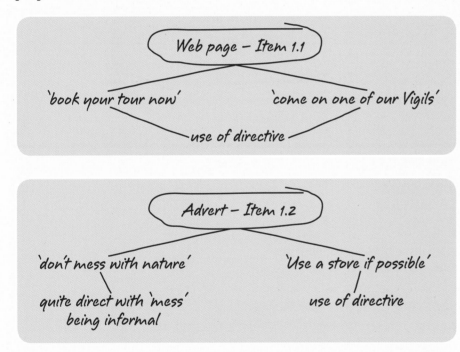

Web page – Item 1.1

'book your tour now'   'come on one of our Vigils'

use of directive

Advert – Item 1.2

'don't mess with nature'   'Use a stove if possible'

quite direct with 'mess'   use of directive
being informal

This student has noticed that one purpose of both Items is to offer advice or to instruct the reader in some way. Look at how the student attempts the question.

DON'T **MESS** WITH **NATURE**

Hey big man.
If you're careless
with fire, I'll *splat*
on your tent!

If you're camping with
your mates this summer
don't mess with nature.
Here's a few pointers
for you to follow
...or else!

HOW TO CAMP RESPONSIBLY:

LIGHTING FIRES. Never cut down or damage trees. Use a stove if possible. If you must have an open fire keep it small and under control and remove all traces before leaving.

HUMAN WASTE. Carry a trowel and bury your own waste and urinate well away from open water, rivers and burns.

LITTER. Take away all your rubbish and consider picking up other litter as well.

PARKING. Use a designated car park where possible and never block a road or lane, an entrance to a field or a building.

KNOW THE CODE
BEFORE YOU GO

Look at the similarities and differences

The reasons why the items have been written

Compare the purposes of the two Items.

Refers to language technique

Gives an example

Infers and interprets

Gives an example

Key word to show comparison

Key word to show comparison

Both Items 1.1 and 2.1 offer advice or instruct the reader in some way although this purpose is not the only one. In Item 1.1, the web page, the writer aims to persuade the reader but advises too by using a directive such as 'book your tour now' to encourage the reader to make a booking with the company. It is short and to the point and the use of 'now' suggests that the reader should act at once. However, in Item 2.1 the purpose of advising is much more practical such as 'Use a stove if possible'. This is a directive but is presented in a less direct way to the reader when compared with Item 1.1 and 'don't mess with nature' which is pretty direct. It is more of a gentle warning than a suggestion to actually do something at once.

Compares

Key word to show comparison

Key word to show comparison

Refers to language technique

Compares

Infers and interprets

Examiner comment: The student tackles this question successfully.

The student:

- uses supporting examples from each Item
- compares by making the point that both Items have similar purposes
- shows that one Item is more direct than the other
- infers and interprets.

Practice question

3

Compare how both Items aim to persuade.

a Highlight and annotate the key words in the question.

b Jot down your ideas in a spidergram like the one in the example above.

c Use these ideas to write a paragraph of your own.

d Highlight where you think you have:

i compared
ii given examples
iii referred to language techniques
iv inferred and interpreted.

Check your revision

You are now going to find out how well you have understood the work in this chapter. Look again at Item 1.2 on page 11 (a web page for Warwick Castle) and Item 2.2 on page 21 (a leaflet focusing on drinking and driving).

What is the question?

Highlight and annotate each of the following examination questions to show that you understand what you are being asked to do:

- Compare how pictures are presented in both Items to interest the reader.
- Compare the ways in which colour is used for effect in both Items.
- Compare how Items 1.2 and 2.2 are presented for effect.

The skills you need to show

Without looking back in this book, copy the table below and write a quick list of words that you need to remember to use to show that you can compare.

Words that show similarities	Words that show differences

Write a paragraph in answer to this question:

Compare the use of colour in Items 1.2 and 2.2.

Once you have written your answer, highlight the words you have used that show where you have shown similarities and differences.

Making choices

Copy and add further ideas to this table.

Purpose	Item 1.2 – web page	Item 2.2 – leaflet
To argue		
To advise		
To		
To		
To		

Make notes showing how you can tell the purposes of each Item.

Writing an answer

Compare how pictures are presented in both Items to interest the reader.

Remember to:

a Highlight the words that are key to answering the question.

b Make notes and find examples.

c Write your answer making sure that you:

   i   point out similarities and differences

   ii refer to the pictures to support your answer

   iii show that you can infer and interpret how pictures are used to interest the reader.

Exploring campaign material

In your English or English Language examination you will be asked to explore the ideas in a text. This means show that you have understood what the text is about and how meaning is conveyed to you.

Reading for meaning

Activity

1   Read Item 4.1, a piece of campaign material produced by the WWF to help protect orang-utans.

Quickly scan the text to get a sense of it then look at the table below. Match the questions to the correct answer.

Question	Answer
In how many years might the orang-utan be extinct?	To sell as domestic pets
For how many years will a mother stay close to her child?	An estimated 230,000
How many orang-utans were there 100 years ago?	Up to 3
In Java and Bali, what is the estimated number of orang-utans that are being lost each day?	30 years
Why do poachers take baby orang-utans?	6 years

Practice question

1   From Item 4.1 list four problems faced by orang-utans.

Remember, you just find four problems and write them down.

You have probably noticed that you simply had to find the answers from the text in this task. It did not require you to explain in your own words or interpret, just find the answer. The first question in your English or English Language examination will ask you to find information and write it down.

The next type of question wants you to show that you can read between the lines and work out what is implied or suggested but not necessarily said.

Item 4.1

WWF *for a living planet*

A mother can only do so much...

The decimation of forest land exposes orang-utans, making it far too easy for poachers to find, kill or steal them.

Here are the shocking facts

- In the last 20 years Borneo lost an area of orang-utan habitat 8 times the size of Wales.
- 100 years ago there were an estimated 230,000 orang-utans, 10 years ago 115,000, but now less than 62,000 remain in the wild. This number is decreasing very quickly.
- 7 years ago orang-utans lived in 44 forest areas, 4 of these areas have now gone completely and others are severely damaged so that orang-utans now only have 37 left in which to live.
- The orang-utan trade on Java and Bali alone may be contributing to the loss of 1,000 a year, that's up to 3 a day.

Unless we act now there could be no wild orang-utans left within 30 years.

That's why they're desperate for your help

If we don't do something to help now, more baby orang-utans will be taken from their mothers and the orang-utan population will continue on a downward spiral to extinction.

You can help protect the remaining orang-utans. By giving just £2.50 a month or a £30 one-off donation, you can adopt an orang-utan and help them live and breed in the wild ensuring a brighter future for the species.

...sometimes it's just not enough

Orang-utan mothers are among the most caring and protective in the animal world. But there's nothing they can do to protect their babies from the threats of poaching or deforestation. Unless we help them it is predicted that the orang-utan could be extinct in just 30 years.

A mother orang-utan will stay extremely close to her child for the first six years of its life. The mother doesn't let her baby out of her sight, so it won't get lost in the forest. After all, certain areas of forest are bigger than some countries.

However, although mothers will do everything in their power to ensure complete safety for their child, *sometimes it's not enough.*

She won't give up without a struggle

Unfortunately, a lot of orang-utans go through something that can only be described as a mother's worst nightmare – having their child taken from them.

Poachers hunt in the forest, seeking baby orang-utans to sell as cute domestic pets. A mother orang-utan never gives up her child without immense struggle, so she is often killed by the poachers as she tries to protect her child. The irony is, once the poachers have torn the baby

orang-utan from its mother, it will become listless or aggressive so it won't make a loveable pet at all.

Deforestation makes it easier for poachers

Orang-utans now only live in the forests of Sumatra and Borneo. And it's these islands in South East Asia that are under threat, consequently putting the orang-utans' homes in danger. Illegal logging, large-scale commercial palm oil production, and man-made forest fires are all threatening the beautiful rainforest which provides the orang-utans with food and shelter.

How you can help

With your help, WWF can continue to work in protected areas where the orang-utans can live and breed safely. *After all, if there are no forests, there are no homes for orang-utans.* Our latest success, the Heart of Borneo Declaration, was endorsed in January 2007. For the first time ever, a firm commitment to protect these 220,000 square kilometres of equatorial rainforest was made.

Will you help to protect them?

Simply complete the form opposite with a gift of just £2.50 a month or a £30 one-off donation and send it back to us. You don't need a stamp. But, if you do choose to use a stamp, even more of our precious funds will go to protect threatened animals.

And, to help you remember your gift, we'll give you a special print and cuddly toy of your adopted animal. You'll also receive a WWF Adoption Certificate, along with information about them and their species. We'll also give you updates throughout the year with information about your orang-utan and other work WWF is involved in.

President: HRH Princess Alexandra, the Hon Lady Ogilvy KG, GCVO
Chairman: Christopher Ward Chief Executive: David Nussbaum
WWF: the global conservation organisation   WWF.org.uk

This leaflet is printed on paper that is 100% recycled – it comes from waste paper. That is paper that has been used previously – e.g. newspapers, magazines, leftover fibres from paper manufacturers and paper from printing companies.
WWF-UK, Panda House, Wayside Park, Godalming, Surrey GU7 1XR
WWF-UK registered charity number 1081247. A company limited by guarantee number 4016725. Panda symbol© 1986 WWF World Wide Fund for Nature (formerly World Wildlife Fund) WWF registered trademark®.
Printed on recycled paper

Reading between the lines

2 Make notes on the following questions. You are going to infer and **deduce** what you think the writer is saying to the reader:

a 'A mother can only do so much ...' What do you think the heading of the leaflet is really trying to say to the reader?

b 'Unless we help them it is predicted that the orang-utan could be extinct in just 30 years.' What does the writer really mean by using 'we'?

Now look at this student's notes.

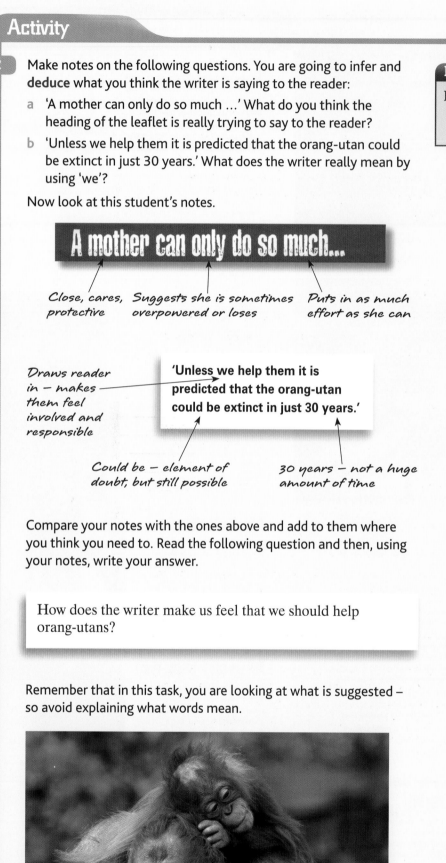

Close, cares, protective

Suggests she is sometimes overpowered or loses

Puts in as much effort as she can

Draws reader in – makes them feel involved and responsible

'Unless we help them it is predicted that the orang-utan could be extinct in just 30 years.'

Could be – element of doubt, but still possible

30 years – not a huge amount of time

Compare your notes with the ones above and add to them where you think you need to. Read the following question and then, using your notes, write your answer.

How does the writer make us feel that we should help orang-utans?

Remember that in this task, you are looking at what is suggested – so avoid explaining what words mean.

Activity cont'd

Now look at these students' attempts at the question. They have been highlighted to show where each is fulfilling the examination mark scheme by inferring, interpreting and deducing – reading between the lines.

Student 1

> We should help the orang-utans because it says that 'A mother can only do so much ...' which means that she can't always look after her child. It also says that 'unless we help them' showing that we need to do something for them.

Student 2

> The writer does not say that we should or must help these animals, but it is obvious that this is what is being suggested. For example, the writer says 'A mother can only do so much ...' that shows that her instinct is to care for and protect her young but 'only' shows that she can be beaten by poachers even if she does 'so much' it might not be sufficient. This makes us see that she will fight for her young but on her own, she is not strong enough so we need to help her. Also, the writer tries to make us feel we should help when he says 'Unless we help them' implying that 'we' as the reader and the charity WWF should stand together to help. The phrase 'could be' makes us think that it is possible that the orang-utan could disappear altogether in a very short amount of time '30 years'. This suggests that things could change quickly unless we get involved.

Student 1	Student 2
Not much is highlighted here as the student does not really infer – they explain what it means rather than what is suggested.	Look at how much is highlighted in this answer – this student is able to show inference very well.
This answer also needs more detail even though the student uses examples.	This student uses words such as 'implying', 'shows', 'suggests' to demonstrate their ability to infer and read between the lines.

Which student's answer would achieve a lower grade and which one a higher grade?

Compare your answer with the two that you have just read. Make a short list of the things that you know you have done well and any things that you think you need to focus on.

Remember:

- use evidence to support your ideas
- *show* what is suggested rather than explain – try to use trigger words such as 'suggests'.

Understanding structure and presentation

3 Look at this smaller version of the whole leaflet.

Now look at the following presentational features that are used in the leaflet and decide where they are used:

- images
- larger font
- text in panel
- bold
- bullet points
- heading
- sub-headings
- logo
- colour.

Remember that the identification of features is a relatively low-level skill. It is the comments that you make about how or why they have been used that gain the marks.

Copy the table below. Focus on just two or three of the presentational features and think about why they are used. Complete the table so that you have a detailed answer in respect of those two or three features. One example has been completed for you.

Presentational feature	Example	Effect of using it
Images	Page 1 – mother and child	Shows happiness, calm and comfort – bond between mother and child
	Page 2 – baby in own habitat	Shows baby washing – looks quiet and peaceful area
	Page 3 – wrecked forest	Shows deforestation – bare, empty, unpleasant place to live, etc.
Larger font		
Text in panel		
Bold		
Bullet points		
Heading		
Subheadings		
Logo		
Colour		

Sample question and answer

Look at how this student takes their ideas and forms them into a structured answer. The highlighted parts show where the student is showing *how* the images involve the reader.

How are images used to involve the reader in the leaflet?

Comments on presentational feature

The image on the cover is large and striking showing a mother and baby orang-utan. The child is cradled in the mother's arms showing that it is loved, protected and cared for. It interests the reader as it suggests a picture of happiness, calm and peace between mother and child. This is added to in the next section where the child is washing itself by a river surrounded by lush green forest showing that the monkeys have both water and shelter and a decent life. However, the third image is of a forest that is bare and empty, showing what humans have done to the natural habitat of the monkeys. This means that it is easier for poachers to find and steal the orang-utans. This final picture is a contrast to the first two to shock the reader and to make them see the difference and want to stop it happening.

Comments on presentational feature

Comments on presentational feature

Practice question

2   Now choose one of the presentational features that you have made notes on and write your own answer to this question:

How is/are _____ used to involve the reader in the leaflet?

Remember to:

- name the presentational feature
- explain how it appears in the leaflet
- comment on *how* and *why* it involves the reader.

Exploring persuasive language

In Activity 3 you examined how to analyse how a text is presented and come up with your own interpretations. In the examination, there will be a question to assess your skills of analysing and exploring the use of language.

Read the following extract from a student's answer. Firstly, the student finds an example from the text and then annotates their ideas. Then they write about how **emotive words** are used for effect in the text. The highlighted parts show where the student has used skills of inference and interpretation.

Key terms

Emotive words: where language is used that appeals to the reader's emotions in order to gain a personal response.

'A mother's worst nightmare'

Most unpleasant, cannot be more horrible than it is

Frightening, trauma, terrifying, dreadful, restless

> Emotive language is used in the text to involve the reader and make them feel sorry for the orang-utans and what they go through. The words 'worst nightmare' are used to shock and disturb the reader. The word 'worst' is used to show that the situation cannot be more horrible and it is the most unpleasant thing for the mother and child to be separated. Also, 'nightmare' shows the fear, trauma and dreadful situations that do happen. The writer deliberately puts 'worst' with 'nightmare' to make the experience of the monkeys being separated sound like an extremely dreadful event. This is to make us feel really sorry for them and to want to stop it for them.

This is a detailed and well-considered answer. Notice that the student:

- selects an appropriate quotation from the text
- analyses and comments on why the words are used
- infers and interprets.

Practice question

3 Find another example of emotive language in Item 4.1 and explore how it has been used for effect. Annotate your ideas and then write your answer. Look back at the example above to help you write your answer.

Compare your answer. Highlight where you have:

- selected an appropriate quotation
- analysed and commented on why the words are used
- inferred and interpreted.

There will be a question in your examination that asks you to look at the language used in one or more Items. To achieve the higher grades, you need to:

- be able to name language techniques
- find and write down examples of them
- explain and comment on why they are used – what effect does the writer want to achieve?

Activity

4 Look at the table below. Column one contains a series of persuasive language techniques. Columns two and three show examples and effects, but these are muddled up.

Match the correct technique to an example and its appropriate effect. One has been done for you.

Persuasive language technique	Example from text	Effect on reader
Emotive words – language that is used to appeal to the reader's emotions	but now less than **62,000** remain in the wild	Shows something at its best
Directly talking to the reader – using words to make the reader feel that the writer is addressing them personally	never gives up her child without an **immense struggle**	Gives an instruction or advice on what to do to help – sometimes a gentle nudge to support the charity
Statistics – numbers and percentages	Will you help to protect them?	Appeals to the reader's emotions by deliberately using words to affect their response – in this case to make us realise how much effort the mother will go to in order to protect her child
Superlatives – words showing something at its best or worst	Simply **complete the form** opposite	The answer is obvious after having read the whole text. The writer is assuming that the reader does not need to offer an answer
Directive – a gentle command or suggestion	orang-utan mothers are among **the most caring**	Uses a number or percentage to show the facts and often to shock the reader
Rhetorical question – a question asked for effect where the answer is obvious	With **your** help, WWF can continue to work	Draws the reader in and makes them feel like the text has been written for them

Remember that in the examination, you will gain more marks by making sure that your answer focuses on the *effects*. That is, why are these techniques used? What impact are they meant to have on the reader?

Often in persuasive texts, a writer will use several techniques in one example. Look at the following quotation that contains both emotive words and statistics to make the point more shocking to the reader.

Emotive language – reduced animals to being sold

Emotive, to suggest something has gone or disappeared

The orang-utan trade on Java and Bali alone may be contributing to the loss of 1,000 a year, that's up to 3 a day.

Statistic and a high number

Statistic to shock, and breaks down 1,000 from a year to a day

Practice question

4 What techniques are used that have an impact on the reader? Annotate the sentences below to show this.

a 'nothing they can do to protect their babies from the threats of poaching'

b 'In the last 20 years Borneo has lost an area of orang-utan habitat 8 times the size of Wales.'

c 'You don't need a stamp. But if you do choose to use a stamp, even more of our precious funds'

Evaluating effectiveness

You might have noticed that this leaflet has been cleverly structured for effect. A writer of a persuasive text has to think carefully about how to gain a reader's attention through the use of language, layout and presentation as well as the order and sequence of the material.

Look at these subheadings from the text (they are in the correct order):

- … sometimes it's just not enough
- She won't give up without a struggle
- Deforestation makes it easier for poachers
- Here are the shocking facts
- That's why they're desperate for your help
- Will you help to protect them?

You probably noticed that the first two subheadings introduce the reader to the orang-utan, but then the third and fourth ones show who and what is making their lives more complicated. The final two subheadings switch to directly addressing the reader to asking for help.

Think about:

- why asking for help from the reader at the start of the leaflet might not work
- why leaving the information about the animals until the end might not be appropriate
- why outlining all of the problems at the start might not be a good idea.

The reader has already got to know the animals at the start and has started to develop an interest in them (the first two subheadings), understood their problems and been given plenty of negative information (third and fourth subheadings). Then they are asked to help change the situation that they are in – by this time they have developed an interest in the orang-utans, seen how their lives are at risk. Next they are asked for a donation to the WWF to help (final two subheadings).

Practice question

5 Now try answering the following question on your own. Aim to write a paragraph looking at how it opens, how it develops and then how it ends.

How has the leaflet been ordered in an effective way?

Look at this student's answer. It shows where they understand how the leaflet has been ordered and that they are able to analyse how it is effective.

> At the start of the leaflet, the writer introduces us to the orang-utan and gives us factual information about how these creatures live. For example, 'A mother orang-utan will stay extremely close to her child for the first six years of its life'. This lets us see how there is a bond between them and we understand that their closeness is similar to ours with our parents when young. The writer then goes on to show how this 'close' relationship is being ruined due to 'illegal logging' and 'man-made forest fires'. Humans are chopping forests down for wood and clearing the vegetation to build on and force the creatures out. This is effective as we have developed an interest in the lives of orang-utans at the start and are now seeing how we as people are ruining their lives. This is meant to make us feel guilty and want to stop it. This then allows the writer to start to ask for our help at the end of the leaflet to stop what man is doing and to allow these animals peace and security. This is very effective as the final thing we read and hopefully remember is that we have the chance to change the situation.

Comments on and understands the structure

Comments on and understands the structure

Comments on and understands the structure

Compare this answer with your own.
- What similarities and differences can you find?
- Have you shown that you can comment on and show understanding of the structure?
- Have you shown inference and deduction when exploring the effectiveness of the order?

Check your revision

You are now going to check that you have understood the key points in this chapter in preparation for your English/English Language examination.

Read the web page campaign material opposite, also produced by the WWF, with the aim of encouraging people to support penguins.

Reading with understanding

List four problems faced by the Adélie penguins in Antarctica.

- Remember that this question tests your literal understanding, so you just need to find four examples and write them down.

Commenting on structure and presentation

How are both pictures and colours used in the web page?

Remember that you need to:

- show that you can infer and interpret
- refer to details in the pictures to support your comments
- think about the colours that are used.

Thinking about language

How does the writer use language to inform and persuade the reader to help WWF and penguins?

Remember that you need to:

- find examples of language to inform and persuade
- give specific examples from the text
- comment on how the language has been used.

Evaluating effectiveness

How effective do you find the WWF web page in encouraging you to help penguins?

Remember:

- this type of question wants you to say what *you* think
- you should give examples to support your points
- you should explain *why* you think it is effective (or not).

Assessment

Use this checklist:

- Reread your answers.
- Highlight in one colour any comments you have made that show inference and interpretation.
- Use another colour to highlight where you have used examples from the text (quotations).
- Use a third colour if you have made any extra comments of your own.

Item 4.2

WWF
for a living planet®

Login

1 Adoption details → 2 Your details → 3 Payment details

Adopt a penguin

Adélie penguins nest and feed on the Antarctic sea ice. But the ice is melting. Help us protect the penguins and their habitats.

How you are helping the penguins

✓ Improving the management of Antarctica's resources and safeguarding its wildlife

✓ Establishing a network of marine protected areas covering at least 10% of the 20 million km^2 Southern Ocean

✓ Reducing illegal and unsustainable fishing practices

✓ Raising awareness of the threats of climate change we all face

Read more about Adélie penguins

Choose a monthly donation

◯ £3 ⦿ £5 ◯ £10 ◯ £ [Other]

This adoption is ⦿ for me ◯ for someone else
(Prefer a one-off payment?)

Your penguin adoption pack will include

A cuddly toy penguin + Updates about your penguin 3 times a year + And loads more fun stuff

Adélie penguins

Adélie penguins live in one of the world's harshest environments, with temperatures reaching -40°c. They can swim up to 4 metres per second and dive to depths of up to 180m.

Location: Antarctic – within the Antarctic Circle
Habitat: Sea ice along the coast and surrounding islands
Wild population: Approximately 2.5 million pairs in 160 colonies

Contact WWF

Please call us on **+44 (0)844 736 0036** (8am-10pm, 7 days a week) if you would prefer to take out your adoption over the phone.

© Sylvia Rubli / WWF-Canon

The threats to Adélie penguins

→ Climate change. Rising global temperatures mean the sea ice is melting, taking away precious nesting grounds and affecting vital food sources such as krill - tiny shrimp-like crustaceans that feed off algae found on the underside of ice sheets.

→ Overfishing. International fishing fleets are plundering fish stocks and removing krill at an alarming rate.

How you are helping the Adélie penguins

✓ £60 (or £5 a month) could pay for helicopter fuel for one hour when tracking penguins across the rugged Antarctic terrain

The penguins of Adélie land

You can adopt five Adélie penguins – a mix of male and female individuals from a colony of 500-600 at the Dumont d'Urville base on Pointe Géologie archipelago, in an area of the Antarctic known as Adélie land. We are monitoring the colony to find out how they are adapting to climate change.

Objectives

In this chapter you will revise:

exploring a personal account

thinking about the ideas

thinking about how the article has been organised

thinking about the ways in which language is used.

Key terms

Personal account: a first-hand description of an experience or event.

Exploring a personal account

In your English or English Language examination you will be asked to explore the ideas in a text. This means show that you have understood what it is about and how this is presented to you.

Reading for meaning

Item 5.1 is a personal account that focuses on a journalist's own experience on 11 September 2001 (the day of the World Trade Center attacks). The account appeared in the *Radio Times* in September 2002, one year after the attacks on the World Trade Center in New York.

Texts containing a personal account often use the five 'W's to begin the writing and orient the reader.

Who? **What?** **Where?** **When?** **Why?**

Activity

1 Complete the five 'W's below by scanning the first part of the account (Item 5.1):

- Who?
- What?
- Where?
- When?
- Why?

The five 'W's form the basis of the whole account.

2 Read the whole article. List four things that the writer clearly remembers happening on 11 September.

Reminder: In this task, which forms the first type of question in the English/English Language examination, you simply need to find and write a list. You do not need to use your own words.

The next style of question tests your ability to infer, deduce and interpret what you have read. This means that you have to show that you can read between the lines.

Think about this question:

How does the writer open the piece in a positive way?

Look at this quotation from the article. A student has highlighted the key words to use in their answer.

'I was in the World Trade Center on that most beautiful of New York mornings, with a serene blue sky and the breeze of early autumn,'

Item 5.1

Wrong place at the right time

A BBC business correspondent was caught up by chance in the catastrophe in New York a year ago – with extraordinary consequences.

I was in the World Trade Center on that most beautiful of New York mornings, with a serene blue sky and the breeze of early autumn, to interview an economist about the chances of recession. (He actually contacted me soon after the devastation to re-arrange the interview that had never happened. I told him that priorities had probably changed).

A year later, I can still feel the impact of the first jet as it went into the North Tower, while I sat in an armchair on the ground floor of the South Tower. It was like a huge, solid door slamming shut, a whoosh of air and the walls vibrating hard in a way that still makes me shudder when a door slams now.

The next two hours were surreal – it's the best word to use. My memories are of focusing on the trivial tasks of reporting (on radio at first via a phone in a hotel room), rather than registering the matters of life and death which seemed utterly unreal then and now. I remember trying to persuade a newsagent

United Airlines Flight 175 crashing into the South Tower of the World Trade Center

to let me use his phone at the foot of the South Tower after the second plane had hit. Stupid though it sounds, I was angry at the phones for not working when the North Tower collapsed and everyone was evacuated from the Embassy Suites Hotel, where I'd hired a room above the line of ambulances leading up to the complex.

The amazing thing about radio reporting is that all you need is a telephone and you really can talk to the world. On September 11, though, I remember presenters in London knew more than I did within minutes because of the amazing television pictures.

I only felt I was in danger once. When the North Tower collapsed, the whoosh of cloud and debris came towards me and I suddenly thought, 'That cloud's moving faster than I can run,' so I turned and fled, ahead of it. Fortunately, my fear was groundless and the debris settled short of me. Until then, I had just assumed these things don't happen in real life.

And that's the feeling still. I still don't really believe it happened. I can't quite believe that those ghastly pictures of the planes crashing into the towers aren't a special effect on celluloid.

People watch in disbelief as the tower burns

Now look at these spidergrams which show the student's thoughts on different ideas suggested by the highlighted words.

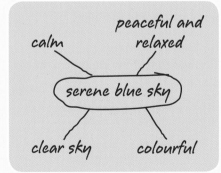

bright   striking

most beautiful of New York mornings

stunning

calm   peaceful and relaxed

serene blue sky

clear sky   colourful

breeze of early autumn

gentle wind

This student has shown that he is able to select the key words from the article and interpret them well. However, this is just like a list. To gain higher grades, the student now needs to use their skills of inference and interpretation to suggest *why* the key words are used. Look at his answer. The highlighted parts show where he does this.

> The writer uses words to show that September 11 began as a spectacular day. He refers to it as the 'most beautiful of New York mornings' suggesting that it is one of the best he has seen as it is striking and bright. He adds to this by referring to the 'serene blue sky' which implies that it is also calm, peaceful and relaxed as the sky is cloudless and colourful. This creates an image of it seeming perfect as though nothing could improve it. He also adds that there was a 'breeze of early autumn' suggesting that there is a gentle wind which is not overpowering.

This answer would achieve a Grade C because it:

- uses examples from the opening of the article
- shows that the student can infer and interpret
- covers three areas to produce a detailed answer.

Practice question

1 Now you are going to answer the following question on your own:

> How does the writer reveal his fear to the reader?

Look at this extract from the article:

> I only felt I was in danger once. When the North Tower collapsed, the whoosh of cloud and debris came towards me and I suddenly thought, 'That cloud's moving faster than I can run,' so I turned and fled, ahead of it.

Look at the student's model answer above and then:

a decide on the *key words* to focus on in your answer

b create a series of *spidergrams* with your initial ideas

c write a *developed paragraph*

d highlight the parts of your answer that show where you have used *inference and interpretation*.

Understanding structure and presentation

When examining structure and presentation in an article that is mainly text, you can still write about:

- how the ideas have been ordered
- the way sentences are structured
- the heading and how it relates to the article
- the pictures and captions and how they relate to the article.

How the ideas have been ordered

The writer is recalling a previous event, his feelings then and his feelings now. The first paragraph of the article is written in the past tense only, but then he starts to move between the past and the present. To do this, he changes tenses frequently. Look again at the first two paragraphs below. The annotations highlight the movements between the past and the present.

> I was in the World Trade Center on that most beautiful of New York mornings, with a serene blue sky and the breeze of early autumn, to interview an economist about the chances of recession. (He actually contacted me soon after the devastation to re-arrange the interview that had never happened. I told him that priorities had probably changed).
> A year later, I can still feel the impact of the first jet as it went into the North Tower, while I sat in an armchair on the ground floor of the South Tower. It was like a huge, solid door slamming shut, a whoosh of air and the walls vibrating hard in a way that still makes me shudder when a door slams now.

Past tense   Present tense

Activity

3   a   Reread the article, highlighting the use of past tense in one colour and the use of present tense in another colour.

b   Which tense does he use in the last paragraph?

The way sentences are structured

Writers often structure sentences in a particular way to achieve a specific effect and to get a reaction from the reader. Look at these sentences from the article:

> A year later, I can still feel the impact of the first jet as it went into the North Tower, while I sat in an armchair on the ground floor of the South Tower. It was like a huge, solid door slamming shut, a whoosh of air and the walls vibrating hard in a way that still makes me shudder when a door slams now.

Now think about this question:

> How does the way the sentences are written show that the writer 'can still feel the impact'?

This question is asking you to focus on *how* the sentences have been structured. What do you notice about:

- the sentence lengths
- the use of commas
- the level of detail?

Look at these ideas jotted down by a student.

> - The sentence lengths – longer complex sentences.
> - The use of commas – add in pauses and separate ideas and details.
> - The level of detail – detailed – many clauses with noun phrases 'huge, solid door' and active verbs 'slamming' and 'vibrating' each adding more to show he 'can still feel the impact'.

This is the beginning of the student's answer to the first two bullet points:

> The writer deliberately structures sentences to show that he 'can still feel the impact' a year later. He uses mainly longer complex sentences in the example to build detail and pack them with vivid description and vital information to reveal his feelings. Moreover, he also uses many commas that add pauses and make the reader build the picture of the scene up bit by bit. This shows that he really 'can still feel the impact' as it is as if he is reliving it again as he is writing.

The highlighted parts indicate where the student is showing evidence of inferring and deducing meaning in the structure of the text.

Practice question

2 Write the final part of the answer by focusing on the last bullet point in the list (about level of detail). Once you have written your answer, highlight the areas where you feel you have inferred and deduced meaning.

Exploring the heading

Headings can have different purposes. They might:
- give a brief outline of the whole story
- use a few words to hint at what the story will be about
- use language techniques to capture the reader's interest.

Look at the heading used in this account:

Wrong place at the right time

Bold used to capture our attention	Contrast in words 'wrong' and 'right' to intrigue the reader	Plays on the familiar phrase: 'right place, wrong time'	Short headline so it stands out and catches the eye

As you can see, there are several points that you can make about a heading.

Practice question

3 Using the ideas annotated below the heading, write a short response to this question:

How has the heading of the personal account been presented for effect?

Reread your answer and highlight where you have inferred and interpreted showing your understanding. The more you can highlight, the higher your grade will be!

Exploring language

So far, you have shown that you can analyse how a text is structured and presented and come up with your own interpretations. In the examination, you will also need to show the examiner that you can analyse and explore the use of language.

Sample question and answer

Read the following extracts from two students' answers. Both are answering the question:

How does the writer use language to involve the reader in the article?

Student 1

He involves us when he uses the word 'shudder' because it shows that he was scared about what was happening and wants us to see this.

Student 2

The writer uses several techniques to involve the reader in the passage as it is an experience that the reader will not have had. For example, he uses onomatopoeia in the word 'whoosh' to give the reader an idea of the force, power and sound of when the planes made an impact. Furthermore, he allows us to share his experience by using a simile 'It was like a huge, solid door slamming shut'. He compares the planes hitting the towers with a massive and heavy door being closed with force and very quickly. This involves us as we can imagine how ferocious the impact was. Similarly, the writer uses emotive language to help the reader picture the destruction caused by the attacks. He uses words such as 'devastation', 'shudder', 'ghastly' as these all give us an idea of how frightening and disturbing it must have been at the scene and that the images were awful.

4 The highlighted parts of the students' answers on page 49 show where they have used skills of inference and interpretation.

What do you notice about the two answers? Think about:

- the level of detail in each one
- the use of examples from the article
- each student's ability to consider the effects achieved by the writer
- which answer would achieve a Grade F
- which answer would achieve a Grade C.

You will have noticed that Student 2 produces a much better answer than Student 1. The first answer only really explains what the words mean without considering the effects. The second answer is more detailed and considers the effects of the language on the reader.

5 In this activity you are going to look in more detail at how language is used for effect.

a Copy and complete the following table. Column one lists language techniques that are used in the article. Column two is for a quotation from the article. Column three is where you interpret and infer why the language technique is used.

Language technique	Example from the article	Comment on why it is used
First person Writing that is personal and from the writer's point of view	I can still feel the impact of the first jet	The first person using 'I' lets the reader know that the account is personal and first hand as the writer is speaking from experience
Emotive language Words that appeal to our emotions or reveal feelings		
Comparisons Comparing one thing or idea with another		
Repetition A word or idea that is repeated over and over		
Noun phrases An object or thing that has at least one or more adjective with it, e.g. compact, new car		

b Highlight the parts of your comment that show you have inferred or interpreted.

Practice question

4 Look at this example from the article and answer the following question by writing a short paragraph.

> And that's the feeling still. I still don't really believe it happened. I can't quite believe that those ghastly pictures of the planes crashing into the towers aren't a special effect on celluloid.

> How does the writer use language to show how incredible the attacks were to him?

Hint: try focusing on particular words, such as the ones highlighted.

Once you have written your answer, check that you have:

- selected a few examples of language from the quotation
- commented on the effects of the writer using these words
- inferred and interpreted meaning.

Evaluating effectiveness

In the exam, you may be asked to evaluate the effectiveness of the presentation and/or language of a text.

In order to evaluate the effectiveness of the language used in the account, look at the following question and example.

Top Tip

The key to doing is well is focusing on your comment about *why* and *how* language is used and the *effects* achieved.

Sample question and answer

> How effective is the writer in showing the danger he felt in this paragraph?

> I only felt I was in danger once. When the North Tower collapsed, the whoosh of cloud and debris came towards me and I suddenly thought, 'That cloud's moving faster than I can run,' so I turned and fled, ahead of it. Fortunately, my fear was groundless and the debris settled short of me. Until then, I had just assumed these things don't happen in real life.

Look at these notes made by a student when planning an answer.

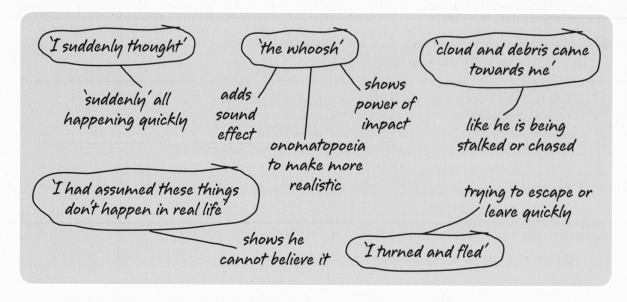

Now read the student's answer. The highlighted parts show where this student is interpreting the effects of the language used.

> The writer is very effective in suggesting the danger that he felt during the attacks. He uses onomatopoeia in the word 'whoosh' to suggest the power and force of the impact to the buildings. This shows that the danger is huge to him. Similarly, he implies that he feels like he is being chased or stalked when he says 'Cloud and debris came towards me' which is also shown when he adds 'I turned and fled' suggesting that he is frightened as he is trying to escape and leave the area quickly. The danger is also effectively shown when he says 'I suddenly thought' which shows that everything is happening quickly and he is having to react quickly too.

Practice question

5   How effective is the writer in showing his feelings in this quotation?

A year later, I can still feel the impact of the first jet as it went into the North Tower, while I sat in an armchair on the ground floor of the South Tower. It was like a huge, solid door slamming shut, a whoosh of air and the walls vibrating hard in a way that still makes me shudder when a door slams now.

Once you have written your answer, highlight where you have explored the effects.

Check your revision

You are now going to find out how well you have understood this chapter.

Read Item 5.2 and complete the activities below, using the bullet points to help you.

Reading with understanding

List four problems caused by the Eurostar train breaking down.

Remember that this question tests your literal understanding, so you just need to find four examples and write them down.

Commenting on structure and presentation

How has the headline been used for effect?

Remember that you need to show that you can infer and interpret.

Thinking about language

How has the writer used language in the first three paragraphs to show his disgust about the situation?

Remember that you need to:

- find examples of language techniques
- give specific examples from the text
- comment on how the language has been used to show the writers disgust.

Evaluating effectiveness

How effective is the writer in making his views about Eurostar clear?

Remember to:

- make your own comments on how effective the article is
- support your ideas with examples from the text
- show that you can infer and interpret.

Assessment

Use this checklist:

- Reread your answers.
- Highlight in one colour comments that show inference and interpretation.
- Use another colour to highlight where you have used examples from the text (quotations).

Item 5.2

Euroscarred

EUROSTAR faces a long haul to restore its reputation after yesterday's report into its pre-Christmas debacle.

The company failed its customers on every level.

Hundreds of passengers were abandoned for hours beneath the Channel, trapped in the dark on airless and stinking carriages.

Five trains broke down because the firm was not prepared for snow in December. Incredibly, no plan existed for an emergency evacuation in the Channel Tunnel.

It was only through the courage of volunteers who took charge that there were no serious casualties.

Thousands had Christmas ruined as all trains were cancelled.

Eurostar chief Richard Brown's admission that 'we let our customers down' must rank as one of the greatest understatements in corporate history.

The firm vows there will never again be such complacency and incompetence.

If it shows it has learned, and focuses relentlessly on safety, Eurostar can win back confidence. That would be good for Britain.

But many passengers have said: 'Never again.' And they mean it.

The Sun Online, 12 February 2010

More about comparison

In order to do well in your English or English Language examination, you need to be able to show that you can compare two texts.

Understanding the question

In the examination you will read and answer questions about three texts. When you get to the final question, you will have to base your answer on two of the three texts. This means that you will be expected to compare them. You will have to choose which two texts you wish to answer questions about.

The final question might look something like this:

Make sure that you only write about two of them *not* three

Now look again at all three Items. They have all been presented in an interesting and effective way.

Choose two of these Items. Compare them using these headings:

Focus on this in a paragraph by comparing

- the titles and subtitles
- the pictures and captions.

Look at how they are set out and organised

Look at the similarities and differences

Compare these features in both texts in a paragraph

You need to read the actual question before you decide which two texts to compare as you need to find the ones that are going to help you write your best answer.

Practice question

1 Look at these questions and make sure that you can underline the key words to show that you understand what to do.

a

Look again at all three Items. Each one has been presented to entertain and interest the reader.

Choose two of these Items. Compare them using these headings:

- the use of colour
- the pictures and diagrams.

b

You are now going to compare two Items out of the three you have read. They have all been organised to interest and involve the reader.

Choose two of these Items. Compare them using these headings:

- the headlines and subheadings
- the use of different fonts and bold text.

Activity

1 Look again at Item 4.1 (page 33), a campaign leaflet produced by WWF focusing on orang-utans, and Item 5.1 (page 45), a personal account of the attacks on 11 September 2001. Remind yourself of the work that you have already done on them.

You are now going to look at how to approach this question:

Look again at Items 4.1 and 5.1. Both have been presented to interest and involve the reader effectively.

Compare them using these headings:

- the headline
- the use of pictures.

Understanding the examiner's mark scheme

Knowing what the examiner is looking for in your answer is an excellent way of understanding how to approach the question. Each of the five questions in your English or English Language examination assesses a different area of reading.

Question number	Assessment focus	Number of marks	What you are being assessed on
1	Retrieval	4	This means being able to find or select information
2	Inference	4	This means reading between the lines – thinking about what is suggested
3	Inference	8	This means reading between the lines – thinking about what is suggested
4	Language	12	This means focusing on how words are used for effect
5	Comparison/ Presentation	12	This means comparing how two texts have been organised and set out on the page

Now let us look at the examiner's mark scheme for Question 5 in the examination. It is marked out of 12. There are three bands, each with different skills. The examiner has to decide which band best fits your answer and then award a mark out of 12.

AO2 iii English / AO3 iii English Language	Skills
Mark Band 3 'clear' 'relevant' 9–12 marks	• Clear evidence that the texts are understood in relation to presentation • Shows clear appreciation and analysis of the effects from the chosen two Items • Offers relevant and appropriate examples from the Items to support ideas • Clear focus on comparisons and cross-references showing how presentation is effective but different between the two Items
Mark Band 2 'some attempts' 5–8 marks	• Some evidence that the texts are understood in relation to presentation • Some appreciation of the effect of the topics from the chosen Items • Attempts to support response with usually appropriate examples • Attempts to compare and make cross-references
Mark Band 1 'limited' 1–4 marks	• Limited evidence that either text is understood in relation to presentation • No real appreciation of the effect of the Items • Very few examples and not well chosen or explained • Limited ability to compare or make cross-references
0 marks	• Nothing worthy of credit

Applying the mark scheme

Activity

2   Read this answer produced in response to the first part of the question focusing on the headings.

Student 1

> Both Items have a headline that is meant to stand out for the reader. They are both short with easy words.

This answer would fall into Mark Band 1 because:

- there is 'limited evidence' of focus on presentation
- there is 'no real appreciation of the effects'
- there are no examples at all
- there is a 'limited ability to compare'.

This answer would probably be awarded 2 out of 12.

What advice would you give Student 1 to improve their answer?

Now read Student 2's answer to the first part of the question focusing on the headings.

- Read the answer.
- Read the mark scheme.
- Apply the mark scheme by trying to find the most suitable mark band and then checking for evidence of each point.

Activity cont'd

Student 2

> Each item starts with a headline to explain what the text is about. Item 5.1 is more catchy as it says 'Wrong place at the right time' so it uses contrasting words in 'wrong' and 'right'. Item 4.1 is far more emotive in its heading as it says 'A mother can only do so much ...' because the words 'mother' and 'only' suggest a struggle. The use of ellipsis is also important as it leaves the reader to think about the rest of the statement and make them continue reading. Both headings are written to make the reader want to know more and to intrigue them.

Student 2 would probably fall into Mark Band 2 as the answer makes 'some attempts'.

- There is 'some evidence' that the student has 'understood presentation'.
- There is 'some appreciation of the effect of headlines'.
- There are 'attempts to support with appropriate examples'.
- There are 'attempts to compare'.

This answer would probably be awarded 6 marks.

3 What advice would you give to Student 2 to improve their answer and move to Mark Band 3?

Now you are going to look at how to plan and write an answer that will achieve Mark Band 3 (9–12 marks).

Make notes

To show that you can compare, spend a few minutes making notes on each heading. Look at this student's annotated ideas. By planning what they want to say and placing each heading side by side in their notes, the student is going to produce a better answer as they have thought about it.

Item 4.1 Campaign leaflet	Item 5.1 Personal account
Heading: 'A mother can only do so much … sometimes it's just not enough'	**Heading:** 'Wrong place at the right time'
Annotate Use of ellipsis … to pause and make reader think about rest of heading	**Annotate** Deliberate contrasting language to intrigue reader 'Wrong' and 'right'
	Bold text – larger than rest of text
Simple words so meaning is not unclear	Simple, straightforward words
Short to stand out – catch interest	Short to catch reader's eye
White text on dark green background to stand out	Black text on white background to stand out
Large font to make clear and be noticed	Larger font to stand out as main idea of text

Once the student had made their notes, they highlighted where they could see direct similarities. Then they used their notes to structure their answer. The highlighted parts are where they have shown evidence of fulfilling Mark Band 3 of the examiner's mark scheme.

Mark Band 3 bullet 1 —
Compares —

Mark Band 3 bullet 2 —

Mark Band 3 bullet 2 —

Compares similarities —

> Both texts use effective headings or titles to interest and involve the reader even though they are different types of writing. Both of them use similar ways to catch the reader's interest as they are short with simple words such as 'Wrong place at the right time' to make the texts clear and to the point. Similarly, both texts use a larger font (in comparison with the rest of the text) to show that this is the title and to make them stand out. In Item 4.1 white text is placed on a dark green background to make it really noticeable whereas in Item 5.1 bold, black text is used on a white background. Both texts use contrasting colours to highlight the heading. However, Item 5.1 differs as the writer is emotive in the use of the word 'wrong' but overall is less emotive than the leaflet's heading. In Item 4.1, the writer uses ellipsis '…' to allow the reader a pause to think and to draw the reader in to the topic.

— Compares similarities
Refers to example
Mark Band 3 bullet 3
Compares similarities

Mark Band 3 bullet 2

Compares differences
Mark Band 3 bullet 2
Mark Band 3 bullet 4
Compares differences

Activity

4 What makes this a good answer? Write a short list of ideas.

You have probably written the following on your list:

- The answer is planned and there is clear evidence in relation to presentation (Mark Band 3 bullet 1).
- The student shows clear analysis of the effects (Mark Band 3 bullet 2).
- Offers a relevant example, although only one (Mark Band 3 bullet 3).
- Shows clear focus on comparison – similarities and differences (Mark Band 3 bullet 4).
- Words are used that show that the student is comparing, such as 'both'; 'similarly'; 'however'; 'whereas' (Mark Band 3 bullet 4).

Practice question

2 You are now going to plan and write an answer to the second bullet point of the question (about the use of pictures).

> Look again at Items 4.1 and 5.1. Both have been presented to interest and involve the reader effectively.
>
> Compare them using this heading:
>
> • the use of pictures.

In order to produce a good answer:

- make a quick plan by noting down ideas about the pictures in both texts
- think about using words to show you are comparing
- think about why these pictures are used
- use the model on page 58 to help you write your answer.

Activity

5 If you have access to another student's answer, read it and apply the mark scheme. Write them a list of points that advise how to improve their answer.

Check your revision

You are now going to find out how well you have understood the work in this chapter. Look again at Item 4.2 on page 43 (a web page from the WWF) and Item 5.2 on page 53 (a newspaper report about the problems faced on the Eurostar).

What is the question?

Highlight and annotate each of the following examination questions to show that you understand what you are being asked to do.

> • Compare how headings are presented in both texts to interest the reader.
> • Compare the layout of both Items.

The words you need to remember

Without looking back in this book, write a quick list of words that you need to remember to use to show that you can:

- compare similarities
- compare differences.

Write a paragraph in answer to this question:

> • Compare how the headings are presented for effect in Items 4.2 and 5.2.

Once you have written your answer, highlight the words you have used that show where you have compared.

The skills you need to show

Copy the table below and add further ideas that focus on the purpose of each text:

Purpose	Item 4.2 – web page	Item 5.2 – news report
To inform		
To persuade		
To		
To		
To		

Make notes showing how you can tell the purposes of each text.

Writing an answer

Compare the use of pictures in both Items.

Remember to:

a Highlight the words that are key to answering the question.

b Make notes and find examples.

c Write your answer making sure that you:

   i point out similarities and differences

   ii refer to the pictures to support your answer

   iii show that you can infer and interpret how pictures are used to interest the reader.

Euroscarred

***EUROSTAR* faces a long haul to restore its reputation after yesterday's report into its pre-Christmas debacle.**

The company failed its customers on every level.

Hundreds of passengers were abandoned for hours beneath the Channel, trapped in the dark on airless and stinking carriages.

Five trains broke down because the firm was not prepared for snow in December. Incredibly, no plan existed for an emergency evacuation in the Channel Tunnel.

It was only through the courage of volunteers who took charge that there were no serious casualties.

Thousands had Christmas ruined as all trains were cancelled.

Eurostar chief Richard Brown's admission that 'we let our customers down' must rank as one of the greatest understatements in corporate history.

The firm vows there will never again be such complacency and incompetence.

If it shows it has learned, and focuses relentlessly on safety, Eurostar can win back confidence. That would be good for Britain.

But many passengers have said: 'Never again.' And they mean it.

Making your reading skills count in the exam

Objectives

In this chapter you will revise:

how to get as many marks as you can in the exam.

The essentials

- You are tested on your reading skills in Section A of your GCSE English or GCSE English Language paper. This is worth 20% of your final marks.
- You are advised to spend one hour on Section A.
- You will be expected to read three non-fiction Items and answer a total of five questions.
- First there will be three questions, one on each of the three Items.
- Question 4 will ask you to explore how language is used in one of the three Items.
- Question 5 will ask you to choose two of the three Items and compare how they have been presented and organised. Two ideas will be provided and you should focus on these.
- All questions will be based on the Assessment Objectives (see page 1).
- Keep a close eye on the time. You have one hour for Section A. You need to answer all five questions.
- Look at the table below. It shows you that there are more marks available for Questions 3 to 5 than for Questions 1 and 2. You need to spend more time on Questions 4 and 5 as they are worth 12 marks each.

Each of the five questions in your English or English Language examination assesses a specific area of reading.

Question number	Assessment focus	Number of marks	What you are being assessed on
1	Retrieval	4	Being able to find or select information
2	Inference	4	Reading between the lines – thinking about what is suggested
3	Inference	8	Reading between the lines – thinking about what is suggested
4	Language	12	Focusing on how words are used for effect
5	Comparison/ Presentation	12	Comparing how two texts have been organised and set out on the page

In the exam, you will write your answer on the actual paper in the space provided. You do not have to fill the space. Remember it is the skills that you demonstrate that gains you marks, not the amount that you write.

Here are five examination questions. The marks awarded for each answer are given. The highlighted boxes would not appear on an exam paper. They are there to explain what each question is asking you to do and how the questions are linked to the Assessment Objectives.

Read **Item 1**, an extract from Save the Children website.

1 List 4 problems faced by children after the earthquake.

(4 marks)

Here you are being asked to:
• read and understand a text
• select relevant information.

2 What has made the disaster 'the worst earthquake in 200 years'?

(4 marks)

Here you are being asked to:
• read and understand a text
• read between the lines – think about what is suggested.

Now read **Item 2**, 'The day I flew into HELL', and answer the question below.

3 What reasons can you find in the news feature for the writer saying that she felt like she had 'landed in hell' and 'it's chaos'?

(8 marks)

Here you are being asked to:
• read and understand a text
• read between the lines – think about what is suggested.

Now read **Item 3** – a leaflet by Unicef called 'Promise me I won't be forced to work'.

4 How does the writer use language to make the leaflet persuasive and shocking to the reader?

(12 marks)

Here you are being asked to:
• focus on how words are used for effect
• explain and evaluate how writers use linguistic and grammatical features to achieve certain effects and engage and influence the reader.

Now look again at all three Items. They have each been presented in an interesting and effective way.

5 Choose two of these Items. Compare them using these headings:

The title
The use of pictures
I have chosen Item ___ and Item ___ .

(12 marks)

You have to choose which two Items you are going to use. If you quickly look at the Items, can you see which two would allow you to answer the question in detail? Which Items have the most interesting titles? Which Items have pictures that are interesting and relevant to the text? In this case, it would be easier to write about Items 2 and 3 than Item 1.

Here you are being asked to:
• collate from different sources, making comparisons and cross-references
• explain and evaluate how two texts are organised and set out on the page.

Activity

1 The texts referred to above are printed on the following three pages. Read them closely. Make some brief notes on the answers you would give to each question.

Item 1

About Us | Jobs | Press | Teachers | Contact

Save the Children

Search...

| Home | News | What we do | Where we work | What you can do | Resources | Donate |

Text size − +

CHANGING LIVES
EMERGENCIES
Niger appeal
China earthquake
Mongolia's deadly winter
South Sudan food crisis
Afghanistan Emergency
Chile earthquake
Haiti earthquake
Children's emergency fund
How we respond
What is an emergency?
How you can help
AMBASSADORS

Haiti earthquake

The worst earthquake in 200 years has struck the country. We're already distributing medical and hygiene supplies and food.

The earthquake hit about 10 miles south-west of Port-au-Prince, the densely-populated Haitian capital, leaving up to 200,000 people dead, 300,000 injured and around 800,000 to 1 million people homeless – making it by far the worst disaster in Haiti in over 200 years.

Around half of all homes in the affected areas were damaged or destroyed. The earthquake hit in the afternoon when many children were in school and separated from their families. Many schools collapsed during the tremors.

Hundreds of thousands of children are sleeping in makeshift shelters in temporary camps, and are in dire need of shelter and support. The risk of outbreak of diseases is very high due to the lack of clean water and so many people living so close together in makeshift camps. The rainy season is expected to begin in late March, and is likely to exacerbate the unsanitary conditions.

Thousands of parents were killed during the earthquake, leaving their children alone and scared. Many children became separated from their parents and families due to the chaos created by the disaster. These children are at risk of trafficking, sexual exploitation and serious emotional distress.

Please give now

Support our work by making a donation

DONATE and help save lives

Related links

→ Read our policy brief
→ Act now to drop the debt for Haiti

Latest blogs

→ Haiti: The amazing children of Leogane
Stuart Bamforth | Mon 17 May

→ UK Election night in Haiti
Stuart Bamforth | Tue 11 May

→ Haiti: Where is the safest place to kip tonight?
Stuart Bamforth | Mon 10 May

→ Haiti: Earthquakes, floods and football
Stuart Bamforth | Sun 9 May

→ Haiti: A nation living under plastic sheets
Stuart Bamforth | Fri 7 May

Find out more

Watch Andrise, a nine-year-old Haitian, describe family life since the earthquake.

Explore the home of Judith Louise, whose 15 day old baby was rescued from her collapsed house.

www.savethechildren.org.uk/en/10181.htm

The day I flew into HELL

I arrived in Haiti from the Dominican Republic this morning. I was on one of the only aeroplanes that managed to reach the tiny airport without being turned away.

It's like I've landed in hell. All around me is devastation. The sound of wailing echoes through the air as the walking wounded, young and old, dig through debris with their bare hands, trying to find their loved ones among the carnage.

There are reports of people tearing pipes from walls in a desperate attempt to find water, and scouring the ground for scraps of food in desperation, but I haven't witnessed this.

On Tuesday, January 12, the small Caribbean country suffered a devastating earthquake. The death toll is expected to top 150,000, while thousands of children have been orphaned, and millions more have lost everything they own.

I'm here with Save The Children and we hope to help survivors keep themselves as healthy as possible in these horrific conditions. There's nothing to eat or drink, the risk of disease is growing, and there's no basic sanitation.

As I'm driven towards the capital, Port-au-Prince, the horror of what's happened is worse than I imagined.

The roads are lined with dead bodies. The air is buzzing with flies and thick with the smell of death.

It's hard to describe my feelings. I'm the director of emergency health and nutrition for the charity, and while I've had training to help me cope with these awful disasters, seeing such human suffering is still hard to take.

I'm dropped off at the Save The Children office, which has been damaged by the quake. I'd hoped to be able to assess the situation quickly and get help to where it's needed most. But it's needed everywhere. It's overwhelming.

According to my colleagues, many of the people they work with are missing and we're short of even the most basic supplies like blankets, food and clean water. I've been told that several people I knew from my time here are dead.

Queues of Haitians arrive to see us. Tired and shocked, many have walked for hours in the sweltering heat in the hope of receiving our help. But we only have a little food and water, and no medicine at all. We do what we can, but it's nowhere near enough. I wish we had more to give them at this stage.

In the afternoon, we take a couple of motorbikes into the heart of the capital. We can't drive the truck because of the rubble blocking the roads.

In town, it's chaos. Crowds of injured people wander around, dazed, cut and bleeding. We've heard reports of men and women looting shops, scavenging what's left for food and supplies, although we haven't seen any of that. Still, the air is tight with tension as people struggle to survive.

I'm going to sleep on the floor of a colleague's house that miraculously hasn't been damaged. At least I've got a roof over my head. Millions don't. I'm lucky.

Item 3

The answers

You have one hour in which to read three texts and answer five questions. You need to give focused answers. The following activities will help you to do this.

2 Remind yourself of Question 1 (see below).
Read Item 1 again.

> **1** List 4 problems faced by children after the earthquake.

Below are two students' answers to this question and the examiner's comments on them.

First student

> *1 people homeless*
> *2 separated from their families*

Examiner comment: This student was awarded 2 marks out of a possible 4 simply because they did not read the question properly. They have only given 2 answers instead of 4, meaning they have thrown away 2 marks.

Second student

> *1 schools collapsed*
> *2 the risk of outbreak of diseases is very high*
> *3 the lack of clean water*
> *4 unsanitary conditions*
> *5 parents were killed during the earthquake, leaving their children alone*

Examiner comment: This student was awarded 4 marks out of a possible 4. Notice that they gave 5 answers (all of which are correct), but only the first four answers would have been marked. Avoid wasting time giving more answers than you need to.

3 Remind yourself of Question 2 (see below). Read Item 1 again.

> **2** What has made the disaster 'the worst earthquake in 200 years'?

Below is a student's answer worth 2 marks. The highlighted text shows the skills that were demonstrated.

Haiti earthquake

The worst earthquake in 200 years has struck the country. We're already distributing medical and hygiene supplies and food.

The earthquake hit about 10 miles south-west of Port-au-Prince, the densely-populated Haitian capital, leaving up to 200,000 people dead, 300,000 injured and around 800,000 to 1 million people homeless – making it by far the worst disaster in Haiti in over 200 years.

Around half of all homes in the affected areas were damaged or destroyed. The earthquake hit in the afternoon when many children were in school and separated from their families. Many schools collapsed during the tremors.

Hundreds of thousands of children are sleeping in makeshift shelters in temporary camps, and are in dire need of shelter and support. The risk of outbreak of diseases is very high due to the lack of clean water and so many people living so close together in makeshift camps. The rainy season is expected to begin in late March, and is likely to exacerbate the unsanitary conditions.

Thousands of parents were killed during the earthquake, leaving their children alone and scared. Many children became separated from their parents and families due to the chaos created by the disaster. These children are at risk of trafficking, sexual exploitation and serious emotional distress.

> ★ **Top Tip**
> Remember, you do not need to write in full sentences in your answer to question 1. However, in questions 2 to 5, it is recommended that you write in full sentences in order to gain better marks.

Activity cont'd

> There are several reasons stated in the web page that show that it is the 'the worst earthquake in 200 years'. For example the use of numbers reveals just how many people have been affected by the event, it says: 'up to 200,000 people dead, 300,000 injured and around 800,000 to 1 million people homeless'. These are very high statistics showing the problems that the disaster has created. Similarly, it says that 'Around half of all homes in the affected areas were damaged or destroyed.' meaning that many people have nowhere to live or nothing left at all.

Green shows use of appropriate examples

Pink shows evidence of inference and deduction

> **Examiner comment:** This answer begins well and shows that the student understands the question. They are able to select examples to refer to and make some attempt to infer and read between the lines. They need to add more by extending their answer – perhaps adding another one or two points to reach the full 4 marks.

Try to add a further one or two points to the student's answer in order to score 4 marks.

Now read the answer below that was awarded 4 marks. It starts the same as the last answer but is more detailed and extended.

How similar were your additional points?

> There are several reasons stated in the web page that show that it is the 'the worst earthquake in 200 years'. For example the use of numbers reveal just how many people have been affected by the event, it says: 'up to 200,000 people dead, 300,000 injured and around 800,000 to 1 million people homeless.' These are very high statistics showing the problems that the disaster has created. Similarly, it says that 'Around half of all homes in the affected areas were damaged or destroyed.' meaning that many people have nowhere to live or nothing left at all. This is made worse by the writer saying that the capital of Haiti is 'densely-populated' which means that so many people have suffered. Another reason that it is 'the worst earthquake' is because of the timing as we are told that: 'The earthquake hit in the afternoon when many children were in school and separated from their families'. This makes it worse because parents and children were apart during a frightening event and many have not found each other since. This is made clear when the writer says that: 'Thousands of parents were killed during the earthquake, leaving their children alone and scared.' The word 'thousands' shows that the impact of the earthquake on children is dramatic and shocking.

Green shows use of appropriate examples

Pink shows evidence of inference and deduction

4 Remind yourself of Question 3 (see below). Read Item 2 again.

> **3** What reasons can you find in the news feature for the writer saying that she felt like she had 'landed in hell' and 'it's chaos'?

In order to answer this question well you need to identify and interpret thoughts and feelings. Look at the two examples below.

Highlight both students' answers showing where:

- each one has referred to the text
- each one shows evidence of inferring and interpreting what they have read.

First student

> The writer presents the scene as disturbing and frightening when she says she felt like she had 'landed in hell' and 'it's chaos'. The language she uses is emotive when she refers to the 'devastation', implying that it looks like a war zone as everything is destroyed. She sees the chaos of people who 'dig through debris with their bare hands' suggesting that they are desperate to find survivors and that not enough help is being provided at that point.

Second student

> The writer says that she felt like she had 'landed in hell' because what she saw was so disturbing. She says that all she saw was 'devastation' suggesting that everything had been ruined and wrecked. She also hears the 'sound of wailing' meaning that people are crying for their lost ones or because they are in agony. These sounds, as well as the sights of destruction make it appear like chaos. She sees people who do not look right because they are 'wounded' and they are desperate as they 'dig through debris with their bare hands'. She makes it sound like a war zone when she describes it as 'carnage' and the people are not behaving as they usually would because they are 'scouring the ground for scraps of food in desperation'. Here it seems like chaos and hell as they are on the floor like animals looking everywhere for the smallest piece of food in order to survive.

Having read both answers, which one do you think is worth 7 marks and which one is worth 3 marks?

How can the weaker answer be improved?

The day I flew into HELL

I arrived in Haiti from the Dominican Republic this morning. I was on one of the only aeroplanes that managed to reach the tiny airport without being turned away.

It's like I've landed in hell. All around me is devastation. The sound of wailing echoes through the air as the walking wounded, young and old, dig through debris with their bare hands, trying to find their loved ones among the carnage.

There are reports of people tearing pipes from walls in a desperate attempt to find water, and scouring the ground for scraps of food in desperation, but I haven't witnessed this.

On Tuesday, January 12, the small Caribbean country suffered a devastating earthquake. The death toll is expected to top 150,000, while thousands of children have been orphaned, and millions more have lost everything they own.

I'm here with Save The Children and we hope to help survivors keep themselves as healthy as possible in these horrific conditions. There's nothing to eat or drink, the risk of disease is growing, and there's no basic sanitation.

As I'm driven towards the capital, Port-au-Prince, the horror of what's happened is worse than I imagined.

The roads are lined with dead bodies. The air is buzzing with flies and thick with the smell of death.

It's hard to describe my feelings. I'm the director of emergency health and nutrition for the charity, and while I've had training to help me cope with these awful disasters, seeing such human suffering is still hard to take.

I'm dropped off at the Save The Children office, which has been damaged by the quake. I'd hoped to be able to assess the situation quickly and get help to where it's needed most. But it's needed everywhere. It's overwhelming.

According to my colleagues, many of the people they work with are missing and we're short of even the most basic supplies like blankets, food and clean water. I've been told that several people I knew from my time here are dead.

Queues of Haitians arrive to see us. Tired and shocked, many have walked for hours in the sweltering heat in the hope of receiving our help. But we only have a little food and water, and no medicine at all. We do what we can, but it's nowhere near enough. I wish we had more to give them at this stage.

In the afternoon, we take a couple of motorbikes into the heart of the capital. We can't drive the truck because of the rubble blocking the roads.

In town, it's chaos. Crowds of injured people wander around, dazed, cut and bleeding. We've heard reports of men and women looting shops, scavenging what's left for food and supplies, although we haven't seen any of that. Still, the air is tight with tension as people struggle to survive.

I'm going to sleep on the floor of a colleague's house that miraculously hasn't been damaged. At least I've got a roof over my head. Millions don't. I'm lucky.

Activity

5 Remind yourself of Question 4 (see below). Read Item 3 again.

> **4** How does the writer use language to make the leaflet persuasive and shocking to the reader?

You are advised to choose some examples. It is much better to analyse two or three good examples from the text than to write about ten examples in a superficial way.

Read the following student's answer and identify where they have:

- referred to specific language techniques
- explained how writers use language for effect
- supported their comments with references to the text.

Persuasive

The writer uses a variety of language techniques to make the leaflet both persuasive and shocking to the reader. A pattern of 3 is used to make the reader feel sympathy for the children saying 'Every day, they are often alone, and at risk of hunger and illness.' The emotive word 'alone' suggests that they have nobody to care for them; the word 'hunger' shows that they are neglected and 'illness' implies that the conditions in which they live are very poor. The writer uses repetition of the word 'right' to stress that these children deserve better and that their health, education and treatment are basic things which they simply do not receive.

Shocking

The writer is pretty blunt in the use of language to shock the reader. For example, it says that 'Millions of children, often as young as five, are forced to live on dangerous city streets.' The statistic 'millions' is shocking as this is a very high figure; similarly, their age (5) is disturbing as these children should not be alone at this age. Moreover, 'forced to live on dangerous city streets' is frightening to read as the word 'dangerous' shows how unsafe it is and 'city' makes us think of somewhere huge and scary for young children. The writer goes on to deliberately mention that 'the only way to survive is through prostitution or dangerous work.' because this shows the appalling lives that the children lead. Their options are limited and are meant to upset the reader into donating money.

This student would achieve a mark in the Grade C range. The student has:

- referred to specific language techniques such as a pattern of three and emotive language
- explained how language is used for effect such as 'to stress that these children deserve better and that their health, education and treatment are basic things which they simply do not receive'
- used examples from the text to support their ideas such as 'dangerous'
- addressed the key words in the question, 'persuasive' and 'shocking'.

Choose one other language technique used to persuade *and* shock in Item 3. Write a short paragraph in which you:

- refer to the specific language technique
- examine how the writer uses it for effect
- support your point with an example from Item 3.

6 Remind yourself of Question 5 (see below).

> **5** Choose two of these Items. Compare them using these headings:
>
> - The title
> - The use of pictures.

Read the following answer to the first bullet point.

> Both headings in Items 2 and 3 are deliberately short and to the point to catch the reader's attention and almost shock them into reading on. Both use capital letters to add emphasis and stress key ideas such as 'HELL' in Item 2 and 'FORCED' in Item 3. Both of these words are disturbing and suggest that the rest of the text will be unpleasant in its content. Item 2 is different in that only the word hell is in capitals to show just how different the writer found it from her usual life. In Item 3 the whole heading is in capitals as it is being spoken by a young child and more alarming to read. Items 2 and 3 are both written in the first person using 'I' to show that they are first-hand accounts, 'The day I flew into Hell' and 'PROMISE ME I WON'T BE FORCED TO WORK'. The words 'Promise me' are a plea and this makes it hard for the reader to turn away from the text.

Yellow refers to the Items by quoting from them

Green analyses the effects

Pink compares the items

This student compares well and would be well on their way to gaining a good mark, as they use quotations to support their points, they analyse effects and compare the items.

Using the example that you have just read, write your own comparison of the use of pictures in Items 2 and 3. Remember to:

- use quotations
- analyse the effects
- compare the items.

Highlight your answer like the one above to show where you have fulfilled the Assessment Objectives for the question.

Now that you have worked through a sample paper and learnt how to show your high-level reading skills to the examiner, you are ready to tackle a practice paper on your own.

Check your revision

See how many of these questions about your English or English Language reading examination you can answer without looking back through this chapter:

- How many questions will there be in the reading section?
- How much time do you have for the reading section of the examination?
- How many marks are the first two questions worth?
- In the final question where you have to compare the presentation, how many items do you have to focus on?
- If a question is worth 12 marks, how much time should you spend writing your answer?

Practice examination for the reading section

The questions in the examination are based on the Assessment Objectives.

Here are five examination questions. The marks awarded for each answer are shown. To help you, additional notes are given explaining how the questions are linked to the Assessment Objectives.

Here you are being asked to:
- read and understand a text
- select material appropriate to purpose.

Here you are being asked to:
- read and understand a text
- select material appropriate to purpose.

Read **Item 1**, a blog about going on holiday in space.

1 List 4 points the writer gives for not being able to take a space flight.

(4 marks)

2 How does the writer think the company building the spaceship could spend the money instead?

(4 marks)

Here you are being asked to:
- read and understand a text
- select material appropriate to purpose.

Read **Item 2**, 'Apollo 11: Where were you when the Eagle landed?'

3 How can you tell that the writer found the experience tense and exciting?

(8 marks)

Here you are being asked to:
- explain and evaluate how writers use linguistic and grammatical features to achieve certain effects and engage and influence the reader.

Read **Item 3**, a web page from Virgin Galactic.

4 How does the writer use language to make the web page informative and exciting to the reader?

(12 marks)

Here you are being asked to:
- collate from different sources, making comparisons and cross-references
- explain and evaluate how writers use presentational features to achieve effects and engage and influence the reader.

Now look again at all three Items. They have each been presented in an interesting and effective way.

5 Choose two of these Items. Compare them using these headings:

The titles
The pictures used.

(12 marks)

I have chosen Item _____ and Item _____.

A holiday that's out of this world

23 March 2010, Jane Reynolds

When you were young, did you dream of being an astronaut? Have you ever watched the television footage of Neil Armstrong walking on the moon, and wished it was you? Well, maybe you can and you will. Instead of lying on a beach in the rain, you could be partying on the moon.

When can I go?

Not right now. A company called Virgin Galactic is building a spaceship to take normal people into space. Tickets cost $200,000, but nobody knows when you'll be taking your flight. Oh, and you'll have to spend three days training at the spaceport and pass a medical before you go. And at the moment it is just a flight – to space and back again. No walking on the moon quite yet.

That logo looks familiar ...

Yes, Virgin does run some of the train services in the UK. Some people would argue that they should stop pouring money into space travel and concentrate on getting their trains running on time instead. If you have to catch a Virgin train to work or school every day, you probably think they should make the fares cheaper too.

What do you think? Is space tourism a good idea?

Item 2

Apollo 11: Where were you when the Eagle landed?

John Vidal remembers making giant leaps for mankind on a beach in Gibraltar

Rain-soaked New Yorkers watch Neil Armstrong take his first step on the moon

I was 19, doing a summer job washing cars and delivering beer in Gibraltar. We had no money and had to sleep in Moroccan blankets on the beach.

That night was dead calm, the sky was clear but the moon was not full at all. Forty yards down the beach an American hippy couple had a small transistor radio with a failing battery. Sometime before midnight they cheered loudly when the Eagle landed and we ran over and asked to join them.

So there the four of us sat, yards from the quietly lapping waves, straining to hear the commentary on Voice of America. The astronauts stayed in the Eagle for hours, it seemed. The American girl fell asleep and her boyfriend had to keep waking her.

When Aldrin and Armstrong finally climbed out of the lunar lander we could barely hear anything from the radio, but we howled our heads off and all made giant leaps for mankind in the sand.

Within minutes the battery had failed. When we woke up the moon had disappeared too, and we had to pinch ourselves that any of it had really happened. But two days later we bought a Daily Express and saw photographs, so we knew.

The Dream

After two or three fabulous days of preparing with your crew – you're suited up and you're raring to go. The climb to 50,000 feet is marked with quiet contemplation but there's an air of confidence and eager anticipation.

Then the countdown to release, a brief moment of quiet before a wave of unimaginable but controlled power surges through the craft. You are instantly pinned back into your seat, overwhelmed but enthralled by the howl of the rocket motor and the eye- watering acceleration which, as you watch the read-out, has you traveling in a matter of seconds, at almost 2500mph, over 3 times the speed of sound.

As you hurtle through the edges of the atmosphere, the large windows show the cobalt blue sky turning to mauve and indigo and finally to black. You're on a high; this is really happening, you're loving it and you're coping well. You start to relax; but in an instant your senses are back on full alert, the world contained in your spaceship has completely transformed.

The rocket motor has been switched off and it is quiet. But it's not just quiet, it's QUIET. The silence of space is as awe inspiring as was the noise of the rocket just moments earlier. What's really getting your senses screaming now though, is that the gravity which has dominated every movement you've made since the day you were born is not there any more. There is no up and no down and you're out of your seat experiencing the freedom that even your dreams underestimated. After a graceful mid-space summersault you find yourself at a large window and what you see is a view that you've seen in countless images but the reality is so much more beautiful and provokes emotions that are strong but hard to define.

The blue map, curving into the black distance is familiar but has none of the usual marked boundaries. The incredibly narrow ribbon of atmosphere looks worryingly fragile. What you are looking at is the source of everything it means to be human, and it is home.

Conceptual image:
Virgin Galactic astronaut enjoys Zero G and spectacular views

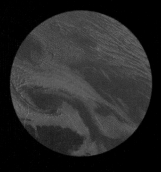

Then you're back to your reclined seat and gravity is starting to return. The deceleration produces strong g forces, but you're lying down easing the intensity. You feel the feathered wings of the spacecraft producing a powerful drag as the thickness of the atmosphere increases, although out of the windows it still looks like space. The g forces quickly ease off and you hear the pilot announce the start of the glide home.

Later that evening, sitting with your astronaut wings, you know that life will never quite be the same again.

Enjoy Zero G
Astrobatics anyone?

Introduction

About the exam

Throughout your GCSE course you have been developing your skills in writing. These skills will help you to cope with the demands of the exam.

There is one exam paper in GCSE English and GCSE English Language. Its focus is: **understanding and producing non-fiction texts**.

Writing is tested in Section B of the paper.

You will be asked to complete two writing tasks: one shorter task worth 16 marks and one longer task worth 24 marks.

You have one hour in which to complete both writing tasks.

This section is worth 20% of your final marks.

The Assessment Objectives

To do well, you need to be clear on what skills are being tested. The Assessment Objectives for your course are printed below. The annotations show you what they mean in terms of the skills you need to show your examiner.

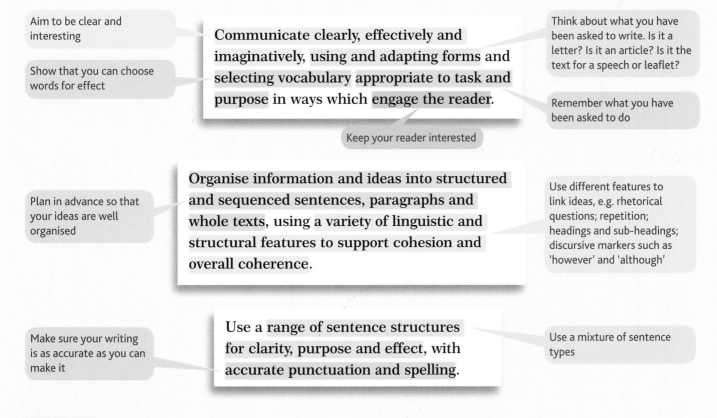

Aim to be clear and interesting

Show that you can choose words for effect

Communicate clearly, effectively and imaginatively, using and adapting forms and selecting vocabulary appropriate to task and purpose in ways which **engage the reader**.

Think about what you have been asked to write. Is it a letter? Is it an article? Is it the text for a speech or leaflet?

Remember what you have been asked to do

Keep your reader interested

Plan in advance so that your ideas are well organised

Organise information and ideas into structured and sequenced sentences, paragraphs and whole texts, using a variety of linguistic and structural features to support cohesion and overall coherence.

Use different features to link ideas, e.g. rhetorical questions; repetition; headings and sub-headings; discursive markers such as 'however' and 'although'

Make sure your writing is as accurate as you can make it

Use a range of sentence structures for clarity, purpose and effect, with accurate punctuation and spelling.

Use a mixture of sentence types

Being prepared

When you take the exam you have one hour to complete the Writing section. This is not a lot of time in which to show your examiner all of your writing skills. The following chapters will help you to understand what is expected and ensure that you show the best of your writing skills in order to gain the most marks.

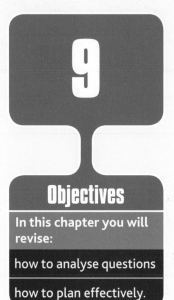

9

Objectives

In this chapter you will revise:

how to analyse questions

how to plan effectively.

Answering the question

Some students do not do as well as they could do in the exam. They make mistakes that could easily be avoided. Student 1, whose writing is reproduced on the next page, was answering the question shown. This was the first task on the Writing paper and the student had 25 minutes in which to complete their answer.

Activity

1 Read the question and the answer on the next page before completing this table to assess what the student did well and what they did not do well.

Skill demonstrated	Level of achievement
The ideas are communicated clearly	some/most/all of the time
The student has written an article	yes/no
The writing is appropriate to the purpose	yes/no
The writing is appropriate to the audience	yes/no
The writing is organised into clear sentences	some of the time/all of the time
The sentences are organised into paragraphs	some of the time/all of the time
There is a range of sentence structures	some range/a good range
There is a range of words chosen for effect	some range/a good range
The spelling and punctuation are accurate	sometimes/usually/always

2 Now compare your assessment with the examiner's. Did you identify similar features?

Examiner comment: The writing is reasonably organised though some paragraphs lack appropriate development. Punctuation and spelling are generally accurate and there is some range in vocabulary and sentence structures. The main problem lies in the content which is not appropriate to purpose or audience. The student was asked to give information about a recent school or college event for other students to read. Instead he has written about the school in general for people who may want to go there.

As the examiner points out, the main problem with the student's response is that they have not written what they were asked to write. The student has not answered the question and their writing is not matched to purpose and audience.

The student would not have made this serious mistake if they had spent a few minutes reading the question and planning the content of their writing.

Top Tip

Make sure you read the question closely and plan your answer.

Sample question and answer

Write an article for a school or college website in which you inform other students about a recent school or college event.

> Welcome to Nestlefield High, the school that aims to make sure that once you've arrived you'll want to stay. This is the most successful school in Birmingham and is one of the most popular. Anybody is welcome. If you come to this school we will guarantee to get you off to a great start in your life.
>
> The school has a great atmosphere, the students are friendly and helpful and the teachers are amongst the best in the country. They take the time to listen to your problems and to really help you with your studies. Many of them are happy to stay behind in the evenings to give you extra help if you need it. It's not surprising that Nestlefield has outstanding exam results and that there is such a high demand for places.
>
> The sporting facilities at Nestlefield are amazing. There are two football pitches, five tennis courts and a running track. There is also a brand new fully equipped gym where you can improve your fitness after school by joining the fitness centre.
>
> The ICT centre is also brand new and you can use the computers during dinner time as well as in your lessons.
>
> If you like the sound of Nestlefield, then I recommend you apply for a place quick. This is because there is limited places and the school is at a high demand because of how successfull it is.
>
> Hope to see you in September!

Planning

Before writing you need to read the question closely and plan your answer to it. Steps A to E below show you what you need to do. In your exam you should spend 4–5 minutes on these steps, so you need to practise.

Step A

Read the question carefully and work out your subject, purpose, audience and the form your writing needs to take.

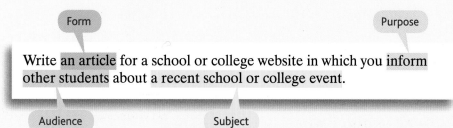

This takes less than a minute, yet many students do not do even this.

Practice question

1 Highlight the subject, purpose, audience and form in each of the following tasks:

- Write a letter to the Chair of Governors at your school or college in which you argue that the school day should be shortened.

- Write the text for a leaflet advising parents on the most effective ways of dealing with their teenage children.

- Write the text for a speech persuading students at your school or college to support the charity of your choice.

Step B

Jot down a range of ideas connected with the subject, for example:

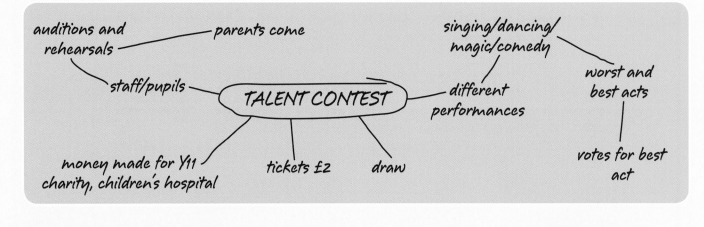

auditions and rehearsals — parents come

staff/pupils

TALENT CONTEST

singing/dancing/magic/comedy

different performances

worst and best acts

votes for best act

money made for Y11 charity, children's hospital

tickets £2   draw

Practice question

2 Choose one of the writing tasks from Practice question 1. Jot down a range of ideas connected with the subject.

Step C

Think about the order in which you are going to place your ideas. Aim to plan three or, at most, four coherent paragraphs. Remember you will only have 20 minutes to write your response. You may think of new things as you do this, for example:

- Para 1: auditions/rehearsals – students + teachers working together
- Para 2: worst and best acts (Marlow's magic/ours)
- Para 3: end of show – votes – winners in draw
- Para 4: money raised – year charity – do it again.

Practice question

3 Using your ideas from Step B, plan 3 or 4 coherent paragraphs. Remember that you do not need to use all of your ideas and you can add new things that you think of.

Top Tip

When planning, select your best ideas and develop them in more detail.

Step D

Remind yourself of the skills that you need to demonstrate in your writing. You need to:

- engage and interest your audience
- use Standard English
- vary your sentence structures
- make sure your meaning is clear
- choose words for effect
- make sure spelling and punctuation are accurate.

Activity

3 Read the list of six bullet points in Step D three times. Close this book and try to write down the six things that you need to do. Check that you have not missed anything out.

Step E

Think of an interesting opening that will engage your readers and start writing, for example:

> The winter term can be the longest and dullest of them all. This year, things were different.

or

> Have you ever wondered what it feels like to be standing on stage in front of 300 people?

or

> The lights went down, the hall fell silent, the curtains opened, and the show began.

When you come to the final sentence of your writing you should aim to end in an interesting way.

Practice question

4 Think of the task you have chosen. Write three possible opening sentences that will engage your readers and choose the best one from these.

Top Tip

Try to avoid using any of the main words from the question in your opening sentence.

4   Choose a different writing task from the selection in Step A. Spend five minutes planning your writing. Make sure you:

- gather a range of ideas
- decide on the order in which you will write about them
- remind yourself of the skills you need to demonstrate in your writing
- think of an engaging opening sentence.

Becoming a good planner

> There is no doubt that good planning makes a significant difference to candidates' marks.
>
> Principal Examiner's Report

Planning puts you in control of your writing. You know where you will start, where you will finish and how you will get from one point to the other. You plan your route.

Before your exam, you need to have developed a way of planning that covers steps A to E above and that works for you. Here are three examples of different students' plans for the question:

> Write an article for a school or college website in which you inform other students about a recent school or college event.

Student A: list

purpose : inform
audience : students
form : article
subject : recent event

school show : Dec 8th

① lead up : preparation / rehearsals

② on the night – tension – behind the scenes – curtain raising

③ the best bits – C's solo – Mr J's magic act

④ applause – lights out – planning

Student B: spidergram

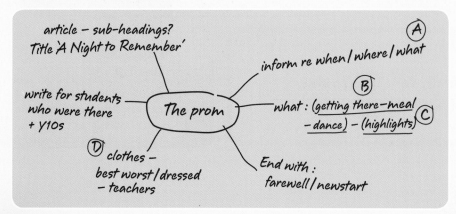

article – sub-headings?
Title 'A Night to Remember'

write for students who were there + Y10s

The prom

Ⓐ inform re when / where / what

Ⓑ what : (getting there – meal – dance) – (highlights) Ⓒ

Ⓓ clothes – best worst / dressed – teachers

End with : farewell / newstart

Student C: ideastorm

> Trip to France
>
> Intro : Normandy – Easter – 25 y11s + 4 teachers – Hist + Lang
> trip – Day 1 : Normandy landings : Day 2 : Bayeaux – Kate + Chris
> got 'lost' – meal in rest. Day 3 : graveyards – feelings / poetry reading
> – Journey there + back – remember to give lots of info and make them
> want to read on. Could do article in diary-type format ?

Which of these plans is closest to the way you like to plan? Is there any way you could improve on it?

Practice question

5 Choose a different writing task from the selection in Practice question 1. Spend five minutes planning your writing. Make sure you plan effectively. Use what you did in Activity 4 as a template.

Writing your answer

You are now almost ready to start writing your answer. There is one last thing you need to remind yourself of – TIME!

This is the short writing task which means that, after planning, you have about 20 minutes in which to write.

Your aim is to produce a complete piece of writing. You may have to leave out something from your plan in order to finish on time. It is better to leave out a point than to run out of time somewhere in the middle. As soon as 15 minutes have passed, start thinking about how you are going to bring your writing to an end. Student A was successful in doing this. Make sure that you are.

5 Using as your guide the plan that you made in Practice question 3, spend 20 minutes writing your answer. Time yourself and keep your eye on the clock!

6 When you have finished writing, assess your writing honestly using the following assessment statements:

a I communicate my ideas clearly some/most/all of the time.

b My writing is/is not appropriate to purpose.

c My writing is/is not appropriate to audience.

d My ideas are sometimes/always organised in controlled paragraphs.

e I have/have not chosen words for effect.

f I have/have not used a range of sentence structures for effect.

g My spelling and punctuation are sometimes/mostly/always accurate.

7 Using your assessment statements, set yourself one target for improvement.

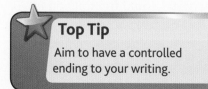

Top Tip

Aim to have a controlled ending to your writing.

Check your revision

Answer the following questions to make sure you have understood the work in this chapter:

- How long should you spend answering the first writing question?
- What should you always do before you start to write?
- About how long should you spend planning an answer?
- What are the five stages of planning?
- What skills do you need to show in your writing?
- What should you do after you have spent 15 minutes writing your answer to the first question?

Objectives

In this chapter you will revise:

how to communicate clearly

how to develop and link your paragraphs.

Key terms

Tone: the mood created through the choice of words.

Slang: words and phrases that are used in an informal context, perhaps when talking with friends.

Standard English: the variety of English most used in public communication, particularly in writing.

Communicating clearly

Getting started

On the front page of your exam paper you are reminded of the 'need for good English'. Remember that even if the question tells you to write for a friend you are also writing for an examiner of English. Your ideas must be clearly expressed so that your meaning is clear to your reader.

However, you can still vary the **tone** of your writing. If you are writing to your local MP your tone is likely to be formal. If you are writing to a friend your tone is likely to be friendly and informal. You should avoid using **slang** or text language and you should write in **Standard English**.

Activity

1   Read the following extracts from students' writing in the exam. Identify where the students have:

● not used Standard English

● not communicated their ideas clearly.

They were all answering this question:

> Write a letter to a friend explaining why you would like him or her to join you in a visit to a place that you think is very special.

Student 1

After that, we could go shopping and buy loads and loads of exciting things to remind us of our stay at Blackpool or you could even win yourself some of the money you have spent in the arcades where there is a brill range of coin machines.

Student 2

If u was to come with me to Bangladesh u will see a place that is very special. I would just love it if u could live with my big, noisy extended family for a while whom I have left behind and come here to Britain which I like very much as well.

Student 3

> We could visit Disneyland, Universal Studios,
> Big Bear town and Hollywood and having all
> these fab places around you will be awesome.
> The city of Los Angeles is great and is different
> to England where we go out shopping at 10am
> and finish at 5pm when everywhere shuts but
> people there and shops are open til about 11pm.

2 Rewrite each of the three extracts in Activity 1 so that the ideas are communicated clearly and in Standard English.

Starting to write

Expressing ideas clearly in Standard English is only the start. You need to make your writing effective so that it will interest your reader from your opening sentence onwards.

About 50 per cent of students start their writing using words from the task. Take for example the task:

> Write a letter to a friend explaining why you would like him or her to join you in a visit to a place which you think is very special.

One student might start like this:

> Dear Reena,
> There is a very special place which I would like you to visit ...

Another might start like this:

> Dear Matt,
> Last year I visited a really special place and I would really like you to join me on a visit there this year ...

And yet another might start like this:

> Dear TJ,
> I am going to explain why I would like you to join me
> on a visit to a place which I think is very special ...

Imagine being an examiner and reading all of these answers that start in very similar ways. Think how refreshing it is to find a student who does something different.

It is not difficult. There are several strategies that you can use. Here are three of them:

- A rhetorical question, for example:

> Dear Reena,
> Do you ever wish you could wake up in an exciting, magical city?

- A series of short sentences, for example:

> Dear Matt,
> This is it. The chance of a lifetime is here. Read on.

- Description, for example:

> Dear TJ,
> Before you read further, just imagine for a moment
> blue skies stretching endlessly above you and the
> warm sun shining on distant mountain tops.

Top Tip

Memorise the three strategies you could use to start your writing: a rhetorical question; a series of short sentences; description.

Activity

3 Using the techniques above, or others that you know of, write two interesting openings for each of the following tasks:

a A group of students from your school or college wants to go on an adventure trip abroad. Write the text of a speech to local business people persuading them to sponsor your group.

b Write an article for parents advising them how to get their children to follow a healthier lifestyle.

For each task, decide which of your opening sentences is most likely to engage the reader.

How to keep your readers' interest

Once you have caught your readers' attention with an interesting opening, you need to keep it. The trick here is to make sure that you develop your ideas in each paragraph and that you link your paragraphs so that the readers can follow your writing easily.

Activity

4 Read the question and answer below. Then complete the table to assess what the student did well and what they did not do well. The student was answering a longer writing task:

> Write an article for a magazine for parents in which you *argue* for or against the idea that there are too many advertisements for sweets on TV.

Do you want your child to have a happy future? Well how the adverts are carrying on you won't. All that's on TV these days are adverts and all that's on adverts are sweets and normally you wouldn't even bat an eyelid on what adverts are on but now it's a growing concern. But what can we do about this?

It's in everybody's daily life. There are billboards when you're on your way to work. As well as that there are magazines when you're at the hairdressers and then most of all, TV.

Just think about when you're walking through Tesco and all your child wants is the latest new Nestle sweet, or a Mars Bar and in the end you give in.

All TV has to do is cut down on the adverts for sweets and change them for fruit. One of the main concerns about this matter is yours and your children's health. You could save so much money from dentists' bills.

I'm not suggesting that your children should cut out sweets altogether. Just cut down. I'm sure your children will live with having sweets just once a week.

Children and stress are linked. And your children are probably watching too much TV and that is going to make them more stressed than ever.

They also get lots of homework to do and this makes them even more stressed and even when they know they should turn the TV off they don't.

Why are adverts on anyway? It didn't used to be as bad when they were only on for a minute. Now they are on for 5 minutes. It's a waste of time. All you have to do now is go to your local Post Office and sign a form. Then hopefully sweets will be banned and you won't have to eat any more of them.

Skill demonstrated	Level of achievement
The student makes a clear attempt to answer the question	yes/no
The student catches the reader's attention in the opening sentence	yes/no
The ideas are communicated clearly	some/most/all of the time
The sentences are organised into paragraphs	some of the time/all of the time
The paragraphs are developed	some/most/all of the time
The paragraphs are linked	some/most/all of the time
The ending is effective and links with the opening	yes/no

5 Now compare your assessment with that of the examiner. Did you identify similar features?

Read the examiner's comments and see if you agree with them.

Examiner comment: This student has made a clear attempt to answer the question. The ideas are usually clearly communicated and she starts well, by immediately addressing the reader and asking a rhetorical question. However, the writing then becomes very disjointed. The sentences appear to be in paragraphs but the paragraphs are not developed. The ideas are not always linked within them and the paragraphs are not always linked with each other. There is no real ending – the student just seems to run out of things to say.

This student's writing is in the Grade D range. To achieve more marks the student needs to:

- aim to write four well-developed paragraphs
- link the ideas within each paragraph
- make clear links between each paragraph and the one that follows it.

Linking and developing paragraphs

In the answer in Activity 4 the student's second paragraph does follow on from the first paragraph by keeping the focus on the reader. However, it is not well developed. We are going to think about how we can use some of the detail in the second, third and fourth paragraphs to write one well-developed paragraph.

The first step is to decide the focus of the paragraph. As the paragraphs are about where you find adverts and the effect that they have on children, we will make this the focus of our paragraph.

Here is what the student wrote:

> It's in everybody's daily life. There are billboards when you're on your way to work. As well as that there are magazines when you're at the hairdressers and then most of all, TV.
>
> Just think about when you're walking through Tesco and all your child wants is the latest new Nestlé sweet, or a Mars Bar and in the end you give in.
>
> All TV has to do is cut down on the adverts for sweets and change them for fruit. One of the main concerns about this matter is yours and your children's health. You could save so much money from dentists' bills.

Here are the paragraphs rewritten as one:

> Adverts are in everybody's daily life. You see billboards when you're on the way to work and there are magazines at your hairdressers which are full of them. It's the same for children. Everywhere they turn they see adverts for sweets, but especially on television. This is why when you go to the supermarket all they want is the latest new Nestlé sweet or a Mars Bar. In the end you give in, but you know this is not good for their health or their teeth. Just think how much money you could save on dentists' bills if TV cut down on adverts for sweets and instead had adverts for fruit!

Notice in the rewritten paragraph:

- each sentence is linked to the one before it
- the paragraph is now appropriately developed.

Now look at the next three paragraphs of the student's answer. The annotations around them give you clues about how you could give your paragraph a clear focus and develop it in detail.

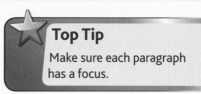

Top Tip

Make sure each paragraph has a focus.

This does not link with the previous paragraph and says nothing about adverts for sweets

> I'm not suggesting that your children should cut out sweets altogether. Just cut down. I'm sure your children will live with less and could just have sweets once a week.
>
> Children and stress are linked. And your children are probably watching too much TV and that is going to make them more stressed than ever.
>
> They also get lots of homework to do and this makes them even more stressed and even when they know they should turn the TV off they don't.

Focus on the link between stress and TV adverts for sweets

Relevant point needs to be made here

To make this a coherent paragraph worthy of Grade C or above, the student needs a focus linked to the question and the paragraph that comes before it. The student could:

- develop the idea of television having fun adverts for fruit
- show the benefits to children of eating more fruit
- end the paragraph with the point that children could still have some sweets.

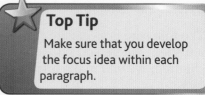

Top Tip

Make sure that you develop the focus idea within each paragraph.

Activity

6 Write a developed paragraph that:
 a is linked with the previous paragraph
 b focuses on adverts for fruit and the benefits of fruit to children's health.

Ending well

It is important to end your piece of writing effectively. You want to leave the examiner with a positive impression of your writing skills. Look again at the student's ending.

> Why are adverts on anyway? It didn't used to be as bad when they were only on for a minute. Now they are on for 5 minutes. It's a waste of time. All you have to do now is go to your local Post Office and sign a form. Then hopefully sweets will be banned and you won't have to eat any more of them.

As the examiner pointed out, this is not a controlled ending – the student just seems to run out of things to say. The first paragraph ended with the rhetorical question: 'But what can we do about this?' The final paragraph could pick up on this by making suggestions. It could suggest that parents:

- monitor what their children watch on TV
- encourage children to do other things
- make sure their children know the benefits of eating fruit.

The first sentence of the answer asks parents: 'Do you want your child to have a happy future?' The final sentence could suggest that if they do these things then their children will have a happy future. This would give the writing a rounded structure and gain the student more marks.

Activity

7 Using the suggestions above to help you, write a final paragraph for this piece of writing.

Check your revision

Answer the following questions to make sure you have understood the work in this chapter:

- What form of English should you use in your writing in the exam?
- Name three techniques that you could use to engage your reader in the opening of a piece of writing.
- Write two pieces of advice for another student on how to write good paragraphs.

Sentence structures and vocabulary

Sentence structures

As you know, there are three main types of sentence.

Simple sentences

These are the first kind of sentences that you learn to write. A simple sentence consists of one main clause that makes complete sense on its own. Simple sentences always contain a subject and a verb. For example:

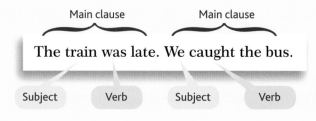

Compound sentences

These have two or more main clauses that are joined by a conjunction such as *and, so, or, but, because*.

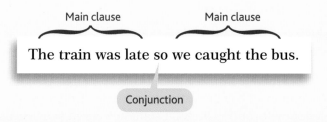

Complex sentences

These have one or more main clauses and one or more subordinate clauses. A subordinate clause does not make complete sense on its own. For example:

Subordinate clause   Main clause

Having realised the train was late, we caught the bus.

Subordinate clause   Subordinate clause

Having realised the train was late, and needing to get home on time, we went to catch the bus but it had been delayed by snow.

Main clause   Conjunction   Main clause

Activity

1 Identify each of the sentences below as simple, compound or complex. Look at the definitions again if you are not sure.

- The girl, who was about 16, walked into the room and smiled at the interviewer.
- The interviewer smiled back.
- She said hello and asked the girl to sit down.
- Before starting the interview, she asked the girl if she would like a cup of tea.

Using a range of sentence structures

No one sentence structure is better than another. There are times when a simple sentence is needed, perhaps for emphasis. At other times a compound or complex sentence is more effective. The important thing is to be able to show your examiner that you can use a range of sentence structures to make your writing interesting.

> **Top Tip**
>
> Aim to show that you can use a mixture of simple, compound and complex sentences for effect.

Activity

2 Compare these two opening paragraphs about a trip to London. Identify:

- the types of sentence used in a
- the types of sentence used in b.

a The taxi arrived. We were waiting for it. The driver took us to the station. We caught the train to London. The station in London was very busy. Then we caught the tube. We arrived in Westminster. Then we took a boat to Greenwich. We met our friends there. The sun was shining brightly.

b We were waiting for the taxi when it arrived. The driver took us to the station and we caught the train to a busy London station, before catching the tube. Having arrived in Westminster, we then took a boat to Greenwich where we met our friends. The sun shone brightly.

Notice how the writer of b has not changed many of the words but has shown the examiner that he can use a range of sentence structures for effect.

Practice question

1 a The following information about London is written in simple sentences. Use the information given here to help you experiment in writing a mixture of simple, compound and complex sentences. You can add or remove details if you wish.

> **London is the capital city of England. London is in south-east England. London has a population of about eight million people. London is the world's ninth-largest city. London is on the banks of the River Thames. The City of London is known as the Square Mile. London was the original settlement of the Romans. The Queen lives in Buckingham Palace in London.**

b When you have written your paragraph, use three colours to highlight your simple, compound and complex sentences.

Changing word order

There are different ways of expressing the same idea.

Look at these different ways of writing:

- John walked down the street to the shop and then returned home.
- Having walked down the street to the shop, John returned home.
- John returned home, having walked down the street to the shop.
- John, having walked down the street to the shop, returned home.

As you can see, by changing the word order, you can put emphasis on different parts of a sentence. You also show your examiner that you are in control of your words and where you place them.

Activity

3 Experiment with the following sentences to find out how many different ways you can write them:

- The little girl lost her doll in the park and cried all the way home.
- They met in an internet chat room and married three years later.
- The sales assistant asked the customers to leave immediately when the fire alarm rang.

Vocabulary

In your exam you should aim to show your examiner that you have a wide vocabulary range. This does not mean that you have to use long and complex words. It means that you must choose the words you use carefully in order to have maximum impact on your reader.

Look at the following examples, which demonstrate how a few changes to vocabulary can add detail and interest to a paragraph.

Answer 1

We were waiting for the taxi when it arrived. The driver took us to the station and we caught the train to a busy London station, before catching the tube. Having arrived in Westminster, we then took a boat to Greenwich where we met our friends. The sun shone brightly.

Answer 2

We were anxiously waiting for the taxi when it finally arrived. The apologetic driver ~~took~~ rushed us to the local station and we just caught the train to a ~~busy~~ crowded and hectic London station, before ~~then~~ catching the tube. Having arrived safely in Westminster, we then took a pleasure boat to Greenwich where we met our friends. The sun shone brightly.

Activity

4 **a** Rewrite the following paragraph by changing and adding words to show you have a wide vocabulary range. In it the student continues to write about their visit to Greenwich.

> The first thing we did was to go to their house and drop off our bags. Then we set off to look around Greenwich. We stopped at a café and had some lunch before going to the market. There were lots of things to see there, including some really good clothes stalls and a toy stall that my brother really liked.

b Highlight the words you have inserted. Do they show that you choose words carefully and have a wide vocabulary range?

Tone

The words you choose can affect the tone of your writing. Tone is the writer's attitude towards the subject and the reader. It can be serious, comic, sarcastic, formal, angry, friendly, and so on.

In the following extract, the student creates a friendly, light-hearted tone. The features of the writing have been annotated for you.

Top Tip

Choose the words you use carefully to add detail and interest and to show that you have a wide vocabulary range.

Uses exaggeration →

> If there's something you really like to do, then it would be a crime not to make use of that in your future choice of career. If you like to cook, then consider a career in catering. If you like to make things then maybe building work or architecture is the way forward for you. If you are good at art, then maybe you should do computer graphics. And, if you like to make money, then maybe you should think about a career as a bank robber! Follow your interest and you can be sure you will find the right job for you.

Addresses the reader directly

Repetition of phrase to appeal to different readers

Uses humour →

In the following extract, the student creates a sarcastic tone, which leaves the reader in no doubt about their opinion. The features of the writing have been annotated for you.

Words that suggest celebration →

Words to suggest pain →

Image to make meaning clear →

> The arrival of this new 'superstar' was greeted with cheers and huge applause from the crowd. But, when she started to sing, the clapping stopped. With a screeching voice, which could halt schoolboys at five paces, she proceeded to torture her captive audience with tune after tuneless tune.

Use of inverted commas to cast doubt on the word

Word that suggests contrast

Play on words to emphasise point

2 **a** Write the opening paragraph of a letter to a local newspaper on a subject of interest to local readers. For example, it could be about:

    i litter on the streets

    ii Christmas lights

    iii the types of shops in the local high street

    iv local sports facilities.

    Your aim is to create a sarcastic tone.

b Now write the opening paragraph of a letter on the same or a different subject. Your aim is to create a friendly tone.

Sentence structure and vocabulary

By using a range of sentence structures and a wide range of vocabulary, you can make a big difference to the grade you get for your writing.

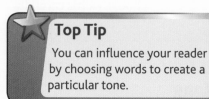

Top Tip

You can influence your reader by choosing words to create a particular tone.

Activity

5 The first paragraph on the next page is how the student you met earlier finished writing about a trip to London. The second paragraph is an improved version.

To help you identify the changes which have been made, copy and complete this table. The first entry has been completed for you.

First version	Improved version
The week was soon over	Sadly, the week was soon over
to go back	
a really good holiday	
and our friends had enjoyed it too	
It was difficult to say goodbye	
really good to	
But we had to go	
another journey by boat	
and then by tube	
and then by train from the station	
when we got back	

Activity cont'd

First version

> The week was soon over and it was time to go back. We'd all had a really good holiday and our friends had enjoyed it too. It was difficult to say goodbye. It would have been really good to stay for longer. But we had to go and that meant another journey by boat and then by tube and then by train from the station. Luckily, we didn't have to wait long for a taxi when we got back!

Improved version

> Sadly, the week was soon over and it was time to return home. We'd all had a brilliant holiday and, fortunately, our friends had also enjoyed it. Saying goodbye was not easy. It would have been fantastic to stay for longer. But we had to leave and that meant another scenic voyage followed by the tube and then, finally, the train from the same crowded station. Luckily, we didn't have to wait long for a taxi when we finally arrived!

> **Top Tip**
> Small improvements can make a big difference to the quality of your writing.

Practice question

3 **a** Write a paragraph of between five and eight sentences about a journey you have taken to go on holiday. Aim to use a range of sentence structures and a wide vocabulary range.

b Look again at the examples above and then at your own writing. Can you make further improvements to show that you can do the following?

  i Use a range of sentence structures.

  ii Use a wide vocabulary range.

If you can, then do.

Check your revision

- What do simple sentences always contain?
- What is the difference between a main clause and a subordinate clause?
- What is a compound sentence?
- What is a complex sentence?
- What kinds of sentence structures should you aim to use in your writing?
- What is your examiner looking for in your choices of vocabulary?
- What is 'tone'?

> **Top Tip**
> Show your examiner that you can use a range of sentence structures and vocabulary.

Objectives

In this chapter you will revise:

punctuation basics

how to use commas

how to spell accurately

how to check your writing.

Technical accuracy

Accuracy in spelling and punctuation is important in an exam that tests your writing skills in English. You need to use everything you have learnt about spelling and punctuation to make sure that, on the day, your writing is as accurate as possible.

In this chapter you will find reminders of some of the basic rules and also tips on what you can do to help you gain a Grade C.

Punctuation basics

Capital letters

Capital letters are used:

- to mark the start of a sentence
- for the word 'I'
- for the first letter of people's names, place names, names of days and months, but not for the names of the seasons such as spring and summer
- for the first letter of the titles of people, such as Mr and Miss
- for some abbreviations and acronyms (US, UNESCO)
- for the main words in the titles of books and films, for example *Lord of the Rings*.

Full stops

Full stops are used to:

- mark the end of a sentence
- show abbreviations (B.Sc. e.g.).

Question marks

Question marks are used to:

- mark the end of a question.

Exclamation marks

Exclamation marks are used to:

- mark shouts or sudden cries, or to show that something is entertaining or worthy of special note.

Activity

1 The following paragraph has been written without capital letters and the ends of sentences have not been marked. Punctuate it correctly.

the future holds many dreams and many worries for all of us i don't know any student who knows what he or she wants to do on leaving school do you there's a part of me which would just like to forget about getting qualifications and a job and travel the world however, i know that if i did that, my mum would kill me and my aunty sarah would probably never talk to me again mr sweeney, my ict teacher, thinks i should try and get taken on by a large computer company such as ibm but i'd need good grades in my gcses so that I could go on and study further

Apostrophes

Apostrophes are used to:

- show where one or more letters have been missed out (omission). The apostrophe is placed in the exact spot where the letter or letters that have been missed out would have been. For example:

we are → we're; I would → I'd

- show that something belongs to someone or something (possession). For example, we might write 'the boy's books' rather than 'the books of the **boy**'. The apostrophe is used to show that the books belong to the boy.

- If we want to shorten 'the books of the **boys**', we place the apostrophe after the 's', as in 'the boys' books' so that our reader knows there is more than one boy.

- If the plural word does not end in 's' we add an apostrophe and 's'. For example:

'the children's books'

Activity

2 The following paragraph should contain four apostrophes to show omission and three apostrophes to show possession. Place the seven apostrophes correctly:

> Louises best friend was planning to go into town on Saturday but Louise wasnt allowed to go with her. Shed asked her mother if she could, but was told she had to stay at home and look after her younger brother, Peter. Peter wasnt too happy about this either. If Louise was there, he wouldnt be able to go to the neighbours house and play with Jason and, more importantly, Jasons new game.

> **Top Tip**
>
> Learn these two commonly used words which do not follow the rule:
> will not → won't
> shall not → shan't.

Inverted commas

Inverted commas (also sometimes referred to as speech marks or quotation marks) are used when:

- a writer uses a speaker's actual words. For example:

"I'm sorry," said the receptionist, "but the doctor is busy."

- a writer is quoting from another text. For example:

Larkin wrote this poem for a newborn girl whom he refers to as a "tightly-folded bud".

Colons

Colons are used to:

- introduce a list. For example:

She packed a bag with the few items she owned: an old pair of jeans, two school shirts, a worn toothbrush and the precious photograph of her sister.

- introduce a lengthy piece of direct speech or a quotation. For example:

He looked her straight in the eye and said: 'This isn't easy for either of us. But we knew, when we started, there would be difficulties ahead.'

This may already seem like a lot to remember, but these are punctuation marks that you have been learning about for many years. Now, you need to make absolutely sure you can use all of them correctly.

3 Rewrite the following sentences using appropriate punctuation:

- kirsty and adam were the most unlikely couple they had met in cranehill secondary school and somehow managed to stay together when all their friends had gone in different directions they had always known their lives would be spent with each other
- this easy walk on the crags above derwentwater in the lake district is quite spectacular early september is the best time for the heather though the great wood, which is owned by the national trust, is worth a visit at any time of year
- stop shouted the guard if you go any further, we will shoot you
- it was his first day at school and he needed to think carefully about what he should take the shiny lizard pencil case, his best batman cape, an apple and his brand-new laser fighter
- havent you got any more money he asked in despair

Punctuation: advanced

Commas

Commas are used to:

- separate items in a list

> If you ever explore this area you will discover that you can go swimming, play football on the green or in the sports centre, visit a range of shops on the High Street and take advantage of the multiplex cinema.

- mark off extra information

> Mr Johnson, a father of four, was unable to show a receipt and Judge Christine Carr, sitting at Lincoln County Court, found him guilty of theft.

- separate a main clause from a subordinate clause

> Although the bus was late, he still got to school on time.

- mark off the spoken words in direct speech

> 'Come with me,' she whispered quietly to the crying child.

You may be wondering why commas appear in the advanced section. You have been learning how to use them for many years. But, it is important for you to know that the correct use of commas within a sentence is a key factor in gaining higher marks.

Commas help the reader to follow the meaning of a text and the examiner will look to see if you can use them correctly.

Activity

4 **a** Place the commas correctly in the following sentences:

    i The fridge contained half a pint of sour milk a lump of mouldy cheese a half-eaten trifle and a tired-looking lettuce.

    ii Imran Qureshi aged 42 and father of three was the first to arrive at the crime scene.

    iii Having closed the door firmly behind her Mrs Bright forgot to turn the key.

    iv He leapt out of his seat as soon as his mother called 'Dinner's ready!'

  b Between now and your exam, whenever you are reading a book, magazine or newspaper, make sure you notice when and how the writers use commas. The best way to learn is through good example.

Spelling: basic rules

Syllables

A syllable is a unit of sound.

A word might contain one syllable (for example 'mud') or many syllables (for example, 'en/ter/tain/ment').

Breaking a word into syllables and sounding each syllable aloud can help you spell the word correctly. For example, saying the word 'diff/i/cult' aloud reminds you of the letter 'i' in the middle.

Prefixes

A prefix is a group of letters that can be added to the beginning of a root word to change its meaning. For example:

Prefixes that are often used include:

disappear → unhappy

> re- mis- in- sub- im- anti- ir- dis-

Once you understand that the prefix is simply added on to the root word, it makes the spelling logical. 'Disappear' only has one 's' because 'dis' is added to 'appear'. 'Irresponsible' has two 'r's because 'ir' is added to 'responsible'.

Suffixes

A suffix is a letter or group of letters that can be added to the end of a root word to change its meaning. For example:

Frequently used suffixes include:

appearing

> -ly -able -ed -ful -ing -ment - ness -ity

In most cases you simply add the suffix to the root word.

However, there are a few exceptions that you need to know. The following list looks long, but these are all things that you will have come across in the past.

Exceptions	Examples
If the word ends in a *c*, add *k* when you add a suffix beginning with *e*, *i* or *y*.	picnic → picnicked
When adding the suffix *-ful* or *-ly* to words that end in a consonant followed by *y*, change the *y* to *i*	plenty → plentiful happy → happily
When a suffix begins with a vowel or a *y* and the root word ends in e, drop the e.	write → writing fame → famous
When a suffix begins with a vowel or a *y* and the root word ends in *ee*, *oe* or *ye*, you keep the final *e*.	agree → agreeable canoe → canoeing
When you add the suffix *-able* to a root word that ends in *ce* or *ge* you keep the final *e*.	notice → noticeable change → changeable
Consonants are usually doubled when you add *-ar*,*-er*, *-ed* or *-ing* to a word that has one syllable and ends with a short vowel and any consonant **except** *y* or *x*.	run → running, beg → beggar play → playing tax → taxed

Understanding how prefixes and suffixes work helps you to be more accurate in your spelling. For example, if you can spell 'satisfy' correctly you should also be able to spell 'dissatisfied', 'unsatisfactory', 'satisfaction' and 'satisfying'.

Activity

5 Use the chart below to help you make as many words as you can using the root words, a prefix and/or one or more suffixes.

Prefix	Root word	Suffix
re	agree	able
mis	inform	ment
im	fair	ly
ir	view	ed
dis	reverse	ful
un	believe	ing
	perfect	ion
	success	ible

Plurals

'Plural' means more than one.

For the vast majority of plural forms you simply add -s to the singular forms.

For example:

book → books   computer → computers

There are some exceptions:

Exceptions	Examples
When the singular form ends in -s, -x, -ch or -sh, add es.	bus → buses tax → taxes church → churches flash → flashes
If a word ends in -y and has a consonant before the last letter, change the y to an i and add es.	party → parties fly → flies
If a word ends in -o you usually just add s. However, there are a few commonly used words that need es to make them plural.	tomato → tomatoes potato → potatoes hero → heroes
If a word ends in -f or -fe you usually change the -f or -fe to –ves.	wolf → wolves knife → knives
There are a few exceptions to the previous rule.	roof → roofs chief → chiefs reef → reefs

There are also some irregular plurals, many of which you will already know. Here are some examples of them:

child → children   man → men   sheep → sheep

mouse → mice   crisis → crises   tooth → teeth

person → people   stimulus → stimuli   goose → geese

Activity

6   Using the rules above, write the plurals of the following words. There are a few irregular words included in the list:

lunch Monday Christmas beach radius lady atlas inch woman blush comedy cactus takeaway hoax stitch ferry bonus plus essay gas arch coach key wish blotch bully doorman hippopotamus medium scissors

Homonyms

Homonyms are words that have the same spelling *or* pronunciation as another, but a different meaning or origin. Here are some homonyms that students frequently mix up:

peace/piece   where/were/wear/we're   their/there/they're

pair/pear   profit/prophet   allowed/aloud   hole/whole

bough/bow   great/grate   ceiling/sealing

7 Choose the correct word to fill the spaces in the following sentences:

a (Where/Were/Wear/We're) going into town (where/were/wear/we're) we are hoping to find something new to (where/were/wear/we're) to the wedding.

b The (profit/prophet) said he would bring (peace/piece) to the land.

c The (hole/whole) of the (great/grate) hall, including the (ceiling/sealing), was bathed in sunshine.

d (Their/There/They're) not (allowed/aloud) to go in (their/there/they're) until (their/there/they're) muddy boots are removed.

In the exam

The important thing to do in the exam is to correct the things you know to be wrong. Take time to look back at the writing you have done for your English over the past few months and make a note of the mistakes you make regularly. These are the things you should look out for in the exam. Never using capital letters for proper nouns or always writing 'I' as 'i' are small errors but annoying ones that you can easily correct.

Top Tip

Always read through your writing and correct errors in punctuation and spelling.

Check your revision

Answer the following questions to make sure you have understood the work in this chapter:

- When should you use inverted commas?
- What are the shortened forms of 'will not' and 'shall not'?
- Complete this sentence: The correct use of _____ within a sentence is often an indicator of a more able student.
- How might counting syllables help you to spell correctly?
- What are prefixes and suffixes?
- Write the plurals of the following words: sheep, crisis, tomato, roof, taxi, fly.

13

Objectives

In this chapter you will revise:

how to write for a particular audience

how to use your best writing skills.

Targeting your audience

So far we have examined the features of good writing, which include:

- answering the question in a planned and organised way
- communicating ideas clearly
- writing in linked and developed paragraphs
- using a varied range of sentence structures
- using a wide range of vocabulary
- punctuating and spelling accurately.

All of these things together will help you to achieve your best grade in English. There is one other thing that you need to remember and that is the person or people you are writing for. Every question will have a stated audience. You need to show you have taken the needs and interests of your audience into account in your writing. Your aim is to interest and engage your reader.

Engaging the reader

The following student was answering a longer writing task. They were expected to get a Grade D. On the day, they used all of their writing skills and exceeded expectations by getting a Grade C. The student's answer on the next page was written in response to this longer writing task:

> Write a letter to a headteacher **arguing** that all students should take part in at least one hour's physical activity every day.

Activity

1   Read the student's plan and answer. You are going to assess it as though you were an examiner. Examiners mark positively. This means they only note the things a student does well that lift them up into a grade boundary. Make a list of the things you think this student does well.

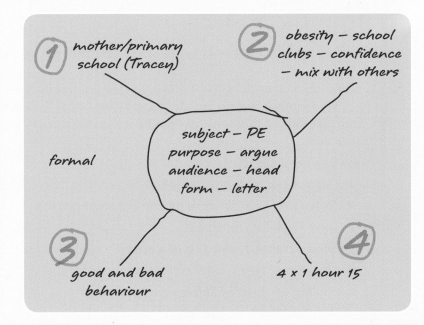

12 Carney Close
Leelham
Bandford
BA24 9SG

10/06/2010

Dear Mr Cooper,

My child Tracey Sleetham has been a pupil at your school for 3 years now. I am extremely happy with her grades, the teachers and everything else in general. However, I am highly appauled at the amount of physical activity they get a week. One hour! No wonder child obesity is a huge issue these days. What do they expect? Luckily I encourage my child to do all of school clubs.

I feel every child would benefit a great deal from putting just one hour a day of activities in place. Firstly, it would help a lot of children who have weight issues to bring there confidence back. Do you feel it's really fair to take away a child's confidence? They are 5–10 years old! They don't know how to look after themselves. That is why they need us. Secondly, it would be a great way for the children to socialise with others and make new friends from other classes. Lastly, it would be a genius way of granting the children a fun reward for excelent behaviour, persuading children to be well behaved throughout the day.

I've thought through my arguement very considerably and understand there will be a few minor obstacles which will occur. For example: how will you find this time? Well, there are four one hour and fifteen minute lessons throughout the day. You could cut the lessons by one fifth which will equal out an hour which you could use for this.

Thank you for your time and I am looking forward to speaking to you very soon.

Yours sincerely

Linda Sleetham

2. Now look at the list below. It shows you the positive features noted by the examiner that earned the student their Grade C. How many of these did you spot? You may not have used the same words as the examiner.

- Engages audience.
- Organised into clear paragraphs.
- Makes a range of points to support argument/purpose.
- Uses vocabulary for effect.
- Shows a range of sentence structures.
- Uses exclamations and rhetorical questions for effect.
- Spelling and punctuation are usually accurate.

Top Tip

When answering a question you can adopt a suitable persona just as this student adopts the persona of a mother.

The first quality that the examiner noted is that the student engages the audience. This means that the student uses a range of methods to draw the reader in. You are going to investigate how they do this. Remember that the reader named in the question is the headteacher.

Activity

3 Annotate the letter to show where the writer does each of the following things to target their audience:

- Addresses the headteacher by name.
- Explains her connection with the school.
- Says positive things about the school.
- Shows that there are benefits for the headteacher.
- Uses a rhetorical question to encourage the headteacher to think about the issue.
- Uses a first-person plural pronoun to put herself and the headteacher on the same side.
- Shows she has considered the issue from the headteacher's point of view.
- Thanks the headteacher for reading the letter.
- Shows that she hopes to speak with the headteacher later.

As you can see, this student constantly had their audience in mind while writing the letter. The student:

- is polite throughout
- balances positives with negatives
- points out the benefits of the argument to the audience
- addresses the audience directly
- considers any difficulties from the audience's point of view.

Top Tip
Always consider the needs of your reader.

Moving up the grades

You are now going to look at another example of a student's writing, who was answering the same question:

Write a letter to a headteacher **arguing** that all students should take part in at least one hour's physical activity every day.

The student adopts a more formal tone and writes as a pupil at the school rather than as a parent. The annotations show you how the student:

- targets their audience
- builds their argument
- uses formal language appropriately.

This student was awarded a mark at the top of Grade C.

28 Markham Street
Burnham
Bandford
BA15 2SX

10/06/2010

Addresses headteacher by name

Dear Miss Johnson,

Explains connection with school

States main argument

I am writing on behalf of myself and several other pupils in Year 11. We wish to propose that all students should take part in at least one hour's physical activity every day. To find out our reasons for this proposal, and why so many people agree with it, please take the time to read on.

Uses appropriate formal language

Polite tone

Makes clear and developed points to support argument

The first and most obvious reason is because of the problem with obesity and affecting the lives of young people. Although, it is not only down to exercise that people will lose weight, one hour's physical activity every day will make a difference in making sure students stay healthy and do not get any serious illnesses from fat related problems. I am sure parents will be very grateful when they realise that you have their children's health and well being at heart.

Shows benefit for the headteacher

Addresses headteacher directly

Makes clear and developed points to support argument

The next reason is that we believe it would relieve the stress of school. Not only will taking an hour out of academic subjects help the pupils relax, but it will also give their brains a much needed rest. This will help them to focus more in their other lessons.

Uses appropriate formal language

Shows benefit for the headteacher

Makes clear and developed points to support argument

In addition, sport can be a great confidence builder. The students will learn to express themselves better, and the team based games will help them develop good communication skills which will be useful when they go to work. This will also be particularly good for pupils who can't go home and run around or play football because they have other responsibilities. This will also benefit the school as pupils will appreciate what you have done for them.

Shows benefit for the headteacher

Addresses headteacher directly

Uses appropriate formal language

Emphasises aim of letter

We hope you will consider our points carefully and will make the right decision so that pupils at your school stay happy and healthy.

Yours sincerely,

Addresses headteacher directly

Kieran Smith

Practice question

1 Use what you have learned from studying the previous students' writing to help you write the opening paragraph of a letter to a headteacher **arguing** that GCSE students should be given two weeks' study leave before their exams.

Aim to:

- address the headteacher directly
- explain your connection with the school
- state your main argument
- use appropriate formal language
- use a polite tone.

Letter layout

The students who answered the previous question were asked to write a letter to a headteacher and have set out their letters appropriately with an address and date at the top. Such letters might be sent by email and generally, in these cases, you just need to provide the greeting, the body of the letter, an appropriate ending and signature. However, sometimes you may be asked to write a letter that will be sent by post, perhaps to a particular business, a politician or to the Chair of Governors at your school. In such cases you will be expected to set your letter out appropriately. Use the template below to help you.

Top Tip

Use language appropriate to your audience.

Writer's full address and postcode. You do not have to use punctuation. If you do, you should be consistent, placing a comma at the end of each line until the last which should have a full stop

The day's date in full

Name (if known), title and address of the intended recipient

Greeting: Dear Sir, Dear Madam or Dear Mr, Ms, Mrs or Miss, followed by the person's surname

Body of the letter with ideas organised into paragraphs

Ending: Yours sincerely (if the recipient is addressed by name), Yours faithfully (if not).

Signature of writer. If the signature is difficult to read, the writer's name should be printed below it

4 Study the template for a formal letter. Then, close this book and sketch your own copy of it from memory. Annotate the different parts. You should annotate seven different elements. When you have finished, check your template to make sure you know how to set out a formal letter.

Practice question

2 Write a letter to a headteacher arguing that students should have the freedom to wear what they want.

Aim to:
- target your audience
- develop your argument
- use formal language appropriately
- use the best of all your writing skills.

You can choose to be a parent or a pupil.

Check your revision

In the next chapter you are going to look at exam questions and how various students have answered them. At different times you will be asked to act as the expert and to make judgements on the quality of the writing. Before you start Chapter 14, look back over all of the work you have revised on writing, including the practice pieces that you have done. Remind yourself of the different areas you have covered and make a list of them. If there are any of these areas that you are not sure about, reread the relevant chapter.

14

Making your writing skills count in the exam

Managing your time

In Section B, the writing part of your exam, you will be asked to do:

- one shorter writing task worth 16 marks

AND

- one longer task worth 24 marks.

The shorter writing task is likely to be more informative or descriptive and be based on personal details and/or experience. In the longer writing task you will be expected to argue, persuade or develop your ideas from a specific viewpoint. Both tasks will ask you to write for an audience and purpose.

You have one hour to complete the writing section. In that hour you need to show the examiner your best writing skills. To make sure you get as many marks as possible, you need to complete both tasks. Aim to spend:

- 25 minutes planning and writing the shorter writing task
- 35 minutes planning and writing the longer writing task.

Plan to write 3–4 paragraphs for the shorter writing task and 4–5 paragraphs for the longer one. There is no point doing one task really well and not leaving enough time for the second one.

Before you continue, look back to page 75 and remind yourself of the skills on which you will be tested. You will be tested on all parts of the Assessment Objectives in each question.

Top Tip

Watch the clock and make sure you answer both writing tasks.

Assessing answers

In this section you are going to read and assess other students' answers to two exam questions. You should use what you learn from this to help you do your best in your own writing in the exam.

Shorter writing task

The following piece by Student 1 was written in response to the following shorter writing task:

> Write a letter to be sent by post to the Prime Minister in which you suggest ways of improving your local area or the country.
>
> *(16 marks)*

The student's answer was placed at the top of the Grade E band.

1

a Read Student 1's answer and assess it using the following criteria based on the Assessment Objectives.

Criteria	Assessment
Is planned well	yes/no
Ideas are communicated clearly	never/sometimes/always
Ideas are logically sequenced	yes/no/sometimes
Has features of a letter	none/some/most
Meets purpose by suggesting ways of improving local area or the country	yes/no/sometimes
Makes a clear attempt to keep the reader interested	yes/no/sometimes
Words are clearly chosen for effect	never/sometimes/often
Vocabulary is varied and sophisticated	yes/no/sometimes
Written in sentences	never/sometimes/always
Shows variety in sentence structures	none/some/a lot
Paragraphs are developed appropriately	never/sometimes/always
Uses devices appropriately (e.g. rhetorical questions, repetition for effect)	never/sometimes/always
Spells simple words accurately	sometimes/mostly/always
Spells complex words accurately	sometimes/mostly/always
Uses a range of punctuation accurately (e.g. full stops, commas, question marks, apostrophes where appropriate)	never/sometimes/mostly

b Choose two areas where you think the most improvement is needed in order to get a higher grade and set two targets for the student with this in mind.

Student 1

> PLAN: Paragraph 1 – introduction   Paragraph 3 – make new point
>   Paragraph 2 – say more about it   Paragraph 4 – ending
>
> Dear Prime minister,
> I am writing to you to give ideas on how to improve the country. At the moment
> it is a discrace with all the litter and the grafiti and there is just not enough good
> transport for people to get around in.
>   The first thing I think you should do is make sure that all the litter gets picked
> up and you could make people who havent got any jobs pick it up or else make
> sure that people have to pay alot of money if they drop it. The second thing I
> think you should do is make sure that there is no more grafiti. At the moment its
> everywhere and it doesnt look good and it looks bad to people who come to this
> country. So I think you should make sure that grafiti is stopped all together and
> dont happen no more. I think that you should make sure that transport is better
> as where I live there just aint no busses at all and people have to use their cars or
> else they just have to walk and that isnt fair on all of the old people who need to
> get to the shops to do their shopping and other stuff like that.
>   yours sincerelly
>   Wei Lin   (E)

Activity

2   Now read the examiner's comments on the student's writing and the targets that the examiner set. Did you identify similar strengths and weaknesses?

> **Examiner comment:**
> **What the student does**
> The student usually communicates their ideas clearly and the ideas are logically sequenced. It has some features of a letter with the salutation and the sign-off and there is an attempt to organise the writing into paragraphs. The student does refer to three distinct areas for improvement and says a little about each of these. They address the reader directly. Spelling of simple words and basic sentence punctuation are usually accurate.
>
> **What the student needs to do to improve**
> The student should aim to improve their planning technique to help them gather and develop ideas before writing. Standard English should be used throughout the letter and a wider, more adult vocabulary range is needed. They should aim to show that they can use a range of punctuation correctly and they need to learn how to use apostrophes for omission. Spelling of more complex words is often inaccurate – spellings such as 'disgrace', 'graffiti', 'buses' and 'sincerely' should be corrected and learnt.

3   Now read the following, much better response to the same task. The student was awarded a mark at the top of the Grade C band.

   a   Using the assessment criteria that you used in Activity 1, identify the ways in which this student's writing is better than that of the previous student.

   b   Write the examiner's comments about what this student does well.

Student 2

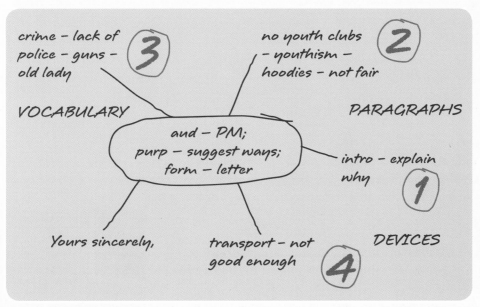

Ivy Cottage
Heatherfield Farm
Danby DO20 5RT

13-06-2010

Dear Prime Minister,

Over the past few years I have noticed that our country is going downhill, and I just wanted to give you a nudge in the right direction as to what to do. I'm sure every member of the public have their own ideas about what's right and wrong, but I'm going to tell you what I, as a young person, think would make a better country.

I'll start with youthism. I think that in the 21st century the elders of the public seem to despise the members of the younger public and label them all as 'hoodies' and 'druggies' and other vile names. But I believe that if we were able to change just this little thing, then, well things could get better. Think of it as laying a foundation. You could start small by just building youth and activity centres. If young people were seen doing good things maybe older people wouldn't call them names.

There are a few other things that bother me. I'll start with the lack of police which is quite simply causing everything to go pear-shaped. As new laws have been introduced, the number of gun crimes and street crimes has increased. The way the police force is run is outrageous; when an elderly lady rings late at night saying there's someone drunk and disorderly outside her house they should be responding immediately, but that just isn't happening.

Just before I finish my letter I just quickly want to say that the quality of public transport is a disgrace and far too over priced. Don't you think that if it's cheaper to get on a train or bus, more people will use one, therefore cutting the CO_2 emissions? If you correct all these faults, I believe that our country could be better and could be one of the higher countries in the continent of Europe.

Thank you,
Yours sincerely,
Daryl Casey

Longer writing task

The answer on the next page was written by Student 3 in response to the following longer writing task. Her answer was placed in the Grade D band.

> Write an article for your school website in which you argue that life is, or is not, too stressful for teenagers nowadays.
>
> (24 marks)

Activity

4 Complete the first column of the following table by listing at least three things the student does well that you think helped them to achieve a Grade D. Complete the second column by listing two or three things that you think prevented them from getting a Grade C.

Set two targets for this student that you think will help them to get a Grade C.

Things the student does well	Things the student does not do well
Targets	

Student 3

> There are many ways in which life is too stressful for teenagers nowadays.
>
> **Clothes**
>
> Clothes and fashion has a big impact on teenagers because teenagers have a lot of peer pressure to look good and wear all the expensive clothes and designer labels. This affects both the teenagers and their parents because it is pressure for their parents if they cannot afford them. This can make their child feel like an outcast if they have to do without when their friends have got all the designer labels.
>
> **Peer pressure**
>
> Some teenagers may have peer pressure from friends to do things they don't want to do like smoke or drink. Therefore this might lead into a teenager doing things that they might not want to do to stay in with what their friends are doing. The pressures on teenagers are very intense today like with drug use which can cause deaths or damage their health and education.
>
> **School**
>
> There is also pressure on teenagers to study more and work a lot harder. They want to achieve good grades but at the same time are pressurised by what they might get. This could cause stress and outbursts to people around them.
>
> The pressures on teenagers having to look good is high and some teenagers can not cope with these expensive pressures in life. Sometimes teenagers are bullied and called names because they have no boyfriends or girlfriends and this might make them feel depression and could affect their school work and social life.

(D)

5 Now read the examiner's comments on the student's work. Did you set the student similar targets to those set by the examiner?

Examiner comment:

What the student does

The writing is organised into sentences and paragraphs and the student matches the writing to purpose and audience most of the time. Whilst there is some variety in sentence structures, they are not always grammatically secure. The student begins to use a range of vocabulary with words such as 'intense' and 'outcast'. Spelling is generally accurate, as is basic sentence punctuation.

What the student needs to do to improve: targets

The student needs to plan the content of each paragraph more carefully before starting to write. This would help them to vary the paragraph openings and make them less repetitive. The student should aim to show a wider, more adult vocabulary range and the ability to structure complex sentences using commas correctly.

6 Now read the following, better response to the same task. This student was awarded a mark at the top of Grade C.

List the ways in which this piece of writing is better than that of Student 3. For each feature you list, select an example from the writing. Record your findings in a table like the one below or annotate the text.

Features of Grade C writing	Example
Avoids repeating question in opening sentence	'Life for teenagers isn't all fun and laughter.'
Makes direct link with reader	'everywhere we turn', 'As soon as we reach', 'straight out to catch us'

Student 4

Life for teenagers isn't all fun and laughter. Young people today are forever trying to avoid the areas of pressure, but everywhere we turn pressure hits us in the face. As soon as we reach the age where people call us 'teenagers', all the stresses of life get bigger and come straight out to catch us. There are just too many to avoid.

Friendships are a large part of most young people's lives. They begin by just talking on the phone but when friends get really close they can be a bad thing rather than a good thing. For example, one friend is taking drugs, so another one does and then it's your turn. At the end of the day everyone knows what the effects of drugs are but even so too many young people turn to drugs as a result of their 'friends'. If you're going to dice with death make sure it's your choice!

Appearance is also a main reason for stress in teenagers today. You're either too fat, too skinny, too short, too tall — the list goes on. Have you ever wondered why nobody ever comments on the good points? Too many people try to change their appearance because of the pressures of TV, media and other people's judgements on them. Girls especially suffer from these things but it affects boys too. Everyone should be allowed to be happy with their own appearance and not wish to look like someone else.

Exams also play an important part in teenagers' stress levels. Family put pressure on them to get good grades, teachers put pressure on them to do the work, schools are always making them think they have to do better and better. A friend of mine is always being told that she should be aiming for an A* and this makes her really nervous and anxious. She's always saying she has to work harder even though she does three hours work every night. It's ridiculous.

So, as you can see life is very stressful for teenagers today. But this is just the beginning. My Mum says not to complain — the stress is much worse when you have teenage children of your own!

Ⓒ

Check your revision

Below you will find the main skills that examiners look for in a student's writing in order to award a Grade C. Look back at the writing of Student 2 and Student 4. Try to identify some or all of these skills in their writing.

Communication

Uses Standard English appropriately

Communicates ideas clearly and with success

Engages the reader

Develops ideas and gives detail

Writes for purpose

Adopts an appropriate tone

Uses a range of language features for effect (e.g. rhetorical questions, lists, repetition)

Uses words effectively (e.g. **discursive markers**)

Organisation

Paragraphs are used effectively

Ideas are linked and structured

Ideas are well thought out

Sentence structure, spelling and punctuation

Writing is grammatically correct

Punctuation within and between sentences is mainly accurate

Uses a range of sentence structures

Spelling of more complex words is usually accurate

Key terms

Discursive markers: words or phrases used to help organise and develop the content, for example: 'in a similar way'; 'nevertheless'; 'although'.

15 Practice examination for the writing section

Here are two questions, typical of the exam you will take. Both questions test the full range of skills. The marks awarded for each answer are also indicated.

You should divide your time according to the number of marks awarded to both tasks. As a rough guide, allow 25 minutes for the first task and 35 minutes for the second task.

> **1** Write a letter to a relative who lives in a different place from you, inviting him or her to visit your home and informing him or her of the different things you could do in your area.
>
> *(16 marks)*
>
> **2** 'Mobile phones should not be allowed in schools.' Write an article for your school website in which you persuade other students that this is a good or a bad idea.
>
> Think about:
> - the advantages of having mobile phones in school
> - the disadvantages of having mobile phones in school
> - how you feel about this issue
> - how to persuade others to agree with you.
>
> *(24 marks)*

Remember:
- Read the questions carefully. Highlight key words to help you work out the subject, purpose, audience and form. Remember, as well as the stated audience, you are always writing for an examiner.
- Spend up to five minutes planning. Gather a range of ideas and decide on the order in which you are going to write about them. Be in control.
- Remind yourself of the writing skills you need to show your examiner.
- Do not repeat the question in your opening sentence. Aim to start in an interesting way that will grab your reader's attention.
- Write in paragraphs and make fluent links within and between them.
- After each paragraph, stop and read what you have written. Make sure it communicates clearly and that you are still addressing the question.
- Aim to use a range of sentence structures to make your writing lively and interesting.
- Aim to use a range of words to interest your reader.
- Keep an eye on the clock so that you have time to complete both tasks.
- Check your writing carefully. Read it 'aloud' in your head. Correct any errors that you spot in punctuation and spelling and make any other improvements.

Answers

Chapter 1: Exploring a web page

Getting started

Activity 1

Any four of:

- Paranormal tours.
- Ghost tours.
- History tours.
- Private tours.
- International tours.
- Events.
- Online shop.
- Workshops.
- Vigils.

Activity 2

a It suggests that:

- they offer a wide range of things to do
- they cater for all types of people and ages
- as a company they are experts on the paranormal.

b 'Engages, Enthrals & Entertains' suggests:

- you will not be bored by what they have to offer
- you will be really interested or absorbed by what they offer
- you will be fascinated and entertained
- you will enjoy it and have fun.

c 'Provides the best' suggests:

- no other company is as good as them
- they cannot be beaten – they are an excellent company.

Referring to details in the text

Activity 3

a The student gives two examples from the web page.

Understanding structure and presentation

Activity 4

The following are possible answers.

a The background scroll; the range of images; the sepia colour; the skeleton hands.

b **i** The background scroll – it looks old fashioned; suggests important information.

　　ii The range of images – this suggests they offer many activities.

　　iii The sepia colour – it hints at the past or history – looking back on the lives of the dead.

　　iv The skeleton hands – they make it seem like you will see the paranormal, they add some humour.

c **i** The background – the scroll, images and skeleton hands are so dominant.

　　ii The text – the whole web page is very visual.

　　iii The bottom of the page – the top half is more visual.

Practice 2

Highlighted parts show inference.

A range of images are used on the web page to not only keep the reader involved but also to suggest the variety of activities that the company offers. Most of the images are linked by history or having a paranormal idea which sums up the main purpose of the company. The Halloween pumpkin is lit up and draws your eye to this part of the page to show that they offer events for this time of year as well as all year round. The skeleton hands are effective as they show that something dead is holding the scroll and this suggests that you might see something similar on one of the tours.

Exploring language

Activity 5

Language technique	Example from web page	Comment on why it is used
Addresses reader directly	When **you** visit Edinburgh	Personalises the text and makes it sound like it is directed specifically at the reader.
Directives	Join a paranormal tour …	Gives a gentle suggestion to the reader to act on what they have read.
Pattern of three ideas	Engages, enthrals & entertains	Shows the company in a positive way – suggests that they offer a service worth paying for.

Evaluating effectiveness

Activity 6

a

Possible purpose	Reasons why you think this might be a purpose
1 To inform the reader about Mercat Tours	There is plenty of factual information showing what they offer.
2 To persuade the reader to book a tour with the company	The company presents itself in a positive way using persuasive words such as 'most spectacular' to make the reader want to book a tour.
3 To frighten people and put them off Edinburgh	Not a purpose – Mercat Tours want people to come to Edinburgh and book a tour with them.
4 To explain the history of Edinburgh	There is some evidence of the history of Edinburgh being mentioned, for example it has a 'dark past', but this is not a major purpose.

i   Purpose 2 is probably the most appropriate as the text is heavily persuasive with plenty of language techniques to achieve this such as:

- superlatives – 'most spectacular'
- pattern of three ideas 'engages, enthrals & entertains'
- directives – 'Book your tour now'.

ii Purpose 3 is the least appropriate as Mercat Tours want people to visit Edinburgh and book one of their tours. They also are aiming their web page at people who want some fun or to be scared by one of their ghost tours.

b

Possible audience	Reasons why you think this might be a possible audience
1 Visitors to Scotland	Mercat Tours is based in Edinburgh – a popular tourist destination in Scotland.
2 Children under the age of five	Not a suitable audience.
3 People who do not believe in ghosts	It does mention people who do not believe ('sceptic') and says that they could perhaps change their mind.
4 People who want a tour that is unique for them	It says that the company can personalise tours to suit your needs.

i Audience 1 is probably the most likely as people tend to do unfamiliar things when visiting new places or holidaying. It could also be audience 4 as a tailored tour would make it special and different for people.

ii Audience 2 is the most unlikely as children under the age of five would genuinely be frightened by the tour and believe that what they see is real. (It does say that the tour features special characters and some that jump out on tour parties.)

Check your revision

Reading with understanding
- Attack and Defence Tour
- The Ghosts of Warwick Castle Tour
- Meet the Falconer
- Go inside the castle
- Visit the castle dungeons.

Commenting on structure and presentation
The main photograph is used to:
- outline one of the things you can see there
- show a re-enactment of a medieval battle
- support the text on the page
- show what arm-to-arm combat looked like
- reveal what war was like in the past.

It suggests that at Warwick Castle you can experience:
- authentic battle scenes making your visit more realistic
- an action-packed day with live fights
- how life might have been at the castle in the past.

Thinking about language

Use of directive to suggest you think

Emotive language – makes it sound like you will be really interested and will enjoy your visit beyond belief

You will not be bored at all

Statistic implies that Warwick Castle has a long history and there will be many things for you to find out and learn about

Emotive word suggesting it is the best or unlike any other castle

Directly addresses the reader and suggests that you will be engrossed throughout the day

Emotive language/noun phrase – makes it sound amazing and beyond belief

Imagine a totally electrifying, full day out at Britain's Ultimate Castle.

Where you can immerse yourself in a thousand years of jaw-dropping history – come rain or shine. Where ancient myths and spell-binding tales will set your imagination alight and your hair on end. Where princesses are pampered and maidens are wooed.

Noun phrases add detail and create a mysterious feel to persuade the reader

Alliteration stresses the point and the choice of words suggest it is also like a fairytale castle

Contrasting words – whatever the weather, Warwick Castle has plenty to offer

Fairytale language adds an element of fantasy to the text

Suggests that the experience will be superb and really interesting

Evaluating effectiveness

- Intended audience – people with an interest in history, battle re-enactments, ghosts and the past, birds of prey.
- Purpose – to inform – to tell you what the castle has to offer; to persuade – plenty of persuasive language; to entertain – references to fairy tales.

Chapter 2: Examining an advert

Getting started

Activity 1

Any four of the following:

- Do not cut down or damage trees.
- Use a stove.
- Keep open fires small and under control.
- Remove fire traces before leaving.
- Bury human waste.
- Do not urinate near open water, rivers or burns.
- Take all of your rubbish with you.
- Use a designated car park.
- Do not block roads/lanes or entrances to fields or buildings.

Activity 2

a   A bird may have been used because:
  - they live in the countryside where people go camping
  - it is easily recognisable.

b   The bird refers to the reader as 'big man' because:
  - humans could ruin the environment where the bird lives
  - humans are bigger than most animals and could harm them
  - it adds some humour.

c   The bird threatens to 'splat on your tent' because:
  - birds tend to 'splat' everywhere
  - it irritates humans when they are 'splat' on
  - it is gentle humour to warn humans about looking after the bird's natural environment.

Referring to details in the text

Activity 3

a   Three times.

Understanding structure and presentation

Activity 4

Focus on presentation and structure	Your ideas
Why do you think a cartoon has been used in the leaflet?	A cartoon is different and may catch the reader's eye more; it also adds humour to a serious topic.
Why is the word 'splat' presented in this way?	It is meant to show what a splat would look like.
Why is the language of the headings slang or informal?	It makes it non-threatening and informal in order to catch the reader's eye even though the topic is serious.
Why is the text presented in short paragraphs?	It keeps the reader alert; it conveys important information quickly and the reader is more likely to read it all.
Why do you think the heading is presented in capital letters?	It stresses the importance of the topic, it highlights the subject of the leaflet.

Practice 2

Highlighted parts show inference and interpretation.

The heading is presented in capital letters to make it stand out and draw the reader in. It is also in capitals to highlight the subject of the leaflet. Furthermore, the words 'mess' and 'nature' are in bold to stress the key ideas of the leaflet and prepare the reader for what is to come in the rest of the text.

Exploring language

Activity 5

a

Language technique	Example from advert	Comment on why it is used
Directives	Take away all your rubbish	A gentle hint or reminder of how the reader can help to protect the countryside.
Use of slang/informal language	camping with your mates	Informal language makes it less threatening and more casual. It also suits a younger audience who might need reminding of how to care for the countryside.
Subject-specific words	damage, traces, waste	The words here relate to the topic under discussion and highlight key points.

Evaluating effectiveness

Activity 6

a

Possible purpose	Reasons why you think this might be a purpose
1 To advise the reader about camping in Scotland	It reminds campers how to protect the countryside and keep it tidy.
2 To persuade young people to be responsible when camping	It offers plenty of advice to help people protect the environment.
3 To warn young people about what could happen to them if they are irresponsible campers	The warning is more humour than a serious threat.
4 To explain how to look after the Scottish countryside	There are plenty of directives to suggest what to do in order to be a responsible camper.

i   Purpose 2 is probably the most appropriate purpose as the leaflet is full of directives and suggestions about how to look after the countryside when camping.

ii Purpose 3 is the least appropriate purpose as a cartoon bird is not even real so cannot make a threat to 'splat' on irresponsible campers. It is said in order to add humour and to keep the interest of the reader.

b

Possible audience	Reasons why you think this might be a possible audience
The general public who go camping	Not really as it is more aimed at a specific audience of young people.
Young people who go camping	This is a suitable audience as the cartoon bird is more suited to a younger reader. The language is more informal and relaxed with words such as 'mates'; 'mess' and 'hey' suggesting that it is aimed at someone younger.
Older people who go camping	Not really as it uses language that is more suited to younger people such as 'mates'.

i The most obvious audience is young people who go camping because:

- the cartoon bird is more likely to attract a younger audience
- there is gentle humour in the bird's speech
- the language is more casual, using words such as 'hey'.

ii The least likely audience is older people because:

- they may be less likely to go camping due to their age
- they are unlikely to go with their 'mates'
- they are less likely to need reminding about looking after the countryside.

Check your revision

Reading with understanding

1 A court conviction.

2 A driving ban of at least 12 months.

3 An endorsement of your driving licence for 11 years.

4 A criminal record.

Commenting on structure and presentation

Images are used in the leaflet for a variety of reasons. Firstly, the background is deliberately blurred to make the text and other images stand out more. It also suggests that drinking alcohol and then driving can affect your vision and distort what you see. It is meant to warn the reader of the risks taken if driving after drinking alcohol. The four bottles are also used to good effect. They show that all types of alcohol can affect your ability to drive, not just wine for example. They also suggest how much some people might drink prior to driving. Moreover, the labels on each bottle have been changed to reinforce to the reader what they could expect if caught drinking and driving. These labels are meant to look authentic but carry important warnings for the reader.

Yellow is inference and interpretation

Blue shows evidence from the Item

Thinking about language

The writer uses language in a variety of ways to make the reader consider the consequences of drinking and driving. For example, the use of the imperative 'So imagine for a moment …' makes the reader start thinking of a scenario suggested by the writer. The writer's use of emotive language such as 'a hefty fine' and 'criminal record' is meant to make the reader think about what could happen if they are caught drinking and driving. The word 'hefty' implies that the fine would be a large sum of money and the word 'criminal' is not one that most people would want attached to them. Moreover, the use of a rhetorical question, 'How will it feel explaining the story of your criminal record at every job interview you go to?' to not only make the reader think but also consider the longer-lasting effects and impact on their life. The writer also cleverly uses the superlative in the example 'even the most basic trip to the cinema' implying that simple events in our everyday lives could be made more difficult as a result of being banned from driving. The word 'most' is intended to stress how inconvenient life would be.

Green shows the techniques used

Blue shows evidence from the text

Yellow is inference and interpretation

Evaluating effectiveness

The leaflet has been presented to be effective in informing people of the consequences of drinking and driving. In this sense, the intended audience is people who both drink alcohol and are able to drive. The purpose is to inform the reader about what happens if you are caught drink driving as well as persuading readers to be more responsible when driving. For example, it says that 'You may also be liable to a fine of up to £5,000 and up to 6 months in prison'. The use of statistics here in the form of a sum of money and period of time are meant to dissuade the reader from driving under the influence of drink. The figure is high and the word 'prison' is intentionally used to put people off taking the risk. This is highly effective in creating the worst case scenario in the mind of the reader. The leaflet also contains suggestions of how to avoid being tempted to drive after drinking and so also instructs and advises the reader. For example, 'Use public transport routes to help you get home'. This advice is meant to be helpful. The writer also personalises the leaflet by referring to the reader directly using the pronoun 'you'. This means that the reader feels like this could in reality happen to them if they are caught drink driving.

Green shows the intended audience and purposes

Pink shows own comments on the effectiveness

Blue shows evidence from the text

Yellow is inference and interpretation

Chapter 3: Making comparisons

Comparing presentation and organisation

Practice 1

a

Look at similarities and differences

Compare how colour is used in both Items.

Write about these two Items

Focus on techniques

The main focus of the task

b

Presentation	Item 1.1	Effect	Item 2.1	Effect
Colour	Sepia Bright colours	Old fashioned, the past Exciting and lively/fun	Pale green Bold background in white and text in black	Countryside colours Contrasting colours more striking

c and d

Colour is used in both items for effect. In Item 1.1, the web page, the colour sepia is used to suggest the past or something old-fashioned or historical. This is effective because the web page is advertising paranormal and ghost tours and therefore the past is important. Other bright colours are used to suggest excitement and fun – such as the lit pumpkin. In contrast, Item 2.1 uses pale green/aqua to reflect the topic of the leaflet which is the countryside. This colour is an important one to use as the whole point of the leaflet is about caring for and protecting the countryside when camping. The contrast between the yellow and red of the lit match suggests the destruction that fire could create. Both items use colours to suit their content but Item 2.1 is more striking as the background colour is white with bold contrasting black text and mainly one other colour whereas Item 1.1 uses a variety of colours making it less striking.

Yellow compares

Green considers effects

Pink infers and interprets

Orange possibly refers to audience and/or purpose

Comparing audience

Activity 2

Possible audience	Item 1.1 – web page	Item 2.1 – advert
Young children		
Teenagers		✓
Parents		
General public	✓	
Retired people		
People who are interested in ghosts	✓	
People who are interested in the countryside		✓

Practice 2

	Discoland	Firland Castle
Use of images	• bright • lively • modern • in circle shape • use of cocktail glass icon to suit audience These all suit a younger audience	• bright • countryside/grounds • in rectangle shape These are more traditional and suit a more mature audience
Presentation	• bold black background highlights images and text in contrasting colours • various fonts for variety • title DISCOLAND made to look light bright flashing lights to suit target audience • capital letters to draw attention • different coloured fonts to add variety and make bright • brief advert • brief use of text	• green background and images reflect peace and calm • scroll effect title suggests tradition or antiquity – suits target audience • simple use of coloured fonts to avoid confusion for older reader • bold for title and opening times etc – key points • brief advert • brief use of text

Green shows similarities

Yellow shows differences

Purpose

Activity 3

a

Look at similarities and differences

Compare the purposes of two Items.

The reasons why the Items have been written

b

Purpose	Item 1.1 – web page	Item 2.1 – advert
To argue		
To advise		✓
To inform	✓	✓
To persuade	✓	✓
To narrate		
To analyse		

Practice 3

a

Look at similarities and differences

Compare how both texts aim to persuade.

Focus on how the writers try to sway your view to theirs

b

Pattern of three with alliteration on E 'Engages, Enthrals & Entertains'

Item 1.1

Superlative – 'best', 'most', 'scariest'

Personal pronouns – 'you', 'your'

Directives 'use a stove if possible', 'consider picking up other litter'

Item 2.1

Emotive words 'responsibly'

Personal pronouns – 'you'

c and d

Both texts aim to persuade the reader but in different ways. Item 1.1 is the most persuasive as it's aim is to encourage people to book a paranormal tour. A range of persuasive techniques are used such as a pattern of three 'ENGAGES, ENTHRALS & ENTERTAINS' which is also an example of alliteration. This is effective as it promotes the tour company in three positive ways suggesting that it will interest, fascinate and be a worthwhile experience for people. Also, the use of alliteration makes it memorable and catches the reader's attention. Similarly, superlatives are used in several places such as 'best', 'most', 'scariest'. These are each effective because they present the company in a very positive way and imply that no other company is as good as them. Finally, another technique used is personal pronouns. Words such as 'you' and 'your' personalise the text and make the reader feel that they are being spoken to directly. This is the same in Item 2.1 where the personal pronoun 'you' is also used to direct the text at the reader. However, Item 2.1 is not as persuasive as it is not trying to sell something but is more advising people on how to care for the countryside. Directives are used often in this text such as 'use a stove if possible' and 'consider picking up other litter' to gently suggest to the reader how to protect the environment when camping. The persuasion here is not as direct as in Item 1.1. Emotive words are used such as 'responsibly' to try to persuade the reader to act in this way. This emotive word links with the superlatives in Item 1.1 but Item 2.1 shows how you can do something good, whereas Item 1.1 shows what would be good for you if you used Mercat Tours.

Yellow compares

Green gives examples

Pink refers to language techniques

Orange infers and interprets

Check your revision

What is the question?

The focus of the question

Look at similarities and differences

- Compare how pictures are presented in both Items to interest the reader.
- Compare the ways in which colour is used for effect in both Items.
- Compare how Items 1.2 and 2.2 are presented for effect.

Look at how they are set out and organised

The skills you need to show

Words that show similarities	Words that show differences
Similarly	However
Also	In contrast
In addition	Alternatively
As well as	On the other hand
In the same way as	
Equally	

Compare the use of colour in Item 1.2 and 2.2

Both items use colours for effect. In the Warwick Castle web page, a bold white background is used with black text to ensure that the page stands out and is easy to follow. White is a traditional colour used for print material and the internet so readers will follow it easily. Similarly, Item 2.2 uses a bold background but this time in black. This is to match the subject of the leaflet which is the consequences of drinking and driving. Black suggests evil and unhappiness and misery so is perhaps used here to signal to the reader the dangers of drink driving. The leaflet also uses bright contrasting colours such as grey and yellow in an information box so that key ideas stand out to the reader. Moreover, the THINK! logo is presented in yellow to stand out. This is the same with the leaflet's title which is bold white with the most important words 'cost you' in yellow to draw attention to the fact that the leaflet is directed at the reader. In contrast, the colours in the Warwick Castle web page are more colourful and varied. This is to imply that the venue is lively and has much to offer. The colours are also important in keeping the reader interested as the web page has quite a lot of text which could be off-putting for some readers.

Highlights show words to indicate similarities and differences.

Making choices

Purpose	Item 1.2 – web page	Item 2.2 – leaflet
To argue	Yes – website implies that it is in a league of its own 'It could only be Warwick Castle'	Yes – the logo advises people to THINK!
To advise		Yes – four bullet points outline problems caused by driving after alcohol
To entertain	Yes – text is packed with many references to events and activities that are lively and engaging	
To inform	Yes – dates, places and times all used to convey information to the reader	Yes – plenty of facts, statistics and time scales to make the consequences clear to the reader
To persuade	Yes – packed with emotive, persuasive and positive language to entice the reader e.g. *'The bravery, skill and agility of the jousters will be tested to the fullest …'* note use of pattern of three ideas, superlative to make it enticing to the reader	Yes – the heading of the leaflet is a rhetorical question to catch interest and imply that drink driving can cost a lot.

Writing an answer

a

look at both – similarities and differences   why and what is used   focus on effects

Compare how pictures are presented in both Items to interest the reader.

the ways in which   the focus of the question

b

Item 1.2 Warwick Castle	Item 2.2 Leaflet
Battle images – bright colours, action-packed and engaging	Blurred and unclear background – dark and mysterious

c Both items use pictures to enhance the text but for different reasons. Item 1.2 is a web page and so is advertising a venue to persuade people to visit. The picture used is placed near the top to add immediate interest and engage the reader as well as outline what the rest of the page is about. A battle image re-enactment is used which is bright and action-packed to suggest excitement and lively activity is on offer at the castle. It gives a glimpse of what people will experience if they visit. However, Item 2.2 is very different. There is no real picture as such, just a blurred and unclear background that is difficult to make out. This is very effective as it is suggesting what the readers' vision could be like when attempting to drive after drinking. It appears mysterious and sinister, perhaps to imply that drinking after driving is a huge risk into the unknown. The pictures in both Items match the content as Item 1.2 is about what you can see and experience whereas Item 2.2 implies the risks and consequences of our actions when drinking and driving.

Similarities and differences

Reference to the pictures

Infer and interpret how pictures are used

Chapter 4: Exploring campaign material

Reading for meaning

Activity 1

Question	Answer
In how many years might the orang-utan be extinct?	30 years
For how many years will a mother stay close to her child?	6 years
How many orang-utans were there 100 years ago?	An estimated 230,0000
In Java and Bali, what is the estimated number of orang-utans that are being lost each day?	Up to 3
Why do poachers take baby orang-utans?	To sell as domestic pets

Practice 1

- They are being poached.
- Adult mothers have their babies taken from them.
- They are sold as domestic pets.
- The adult mothers are often killed fighting to save their babies.
- Their homes are in danger due to deforestation.
- Humans are creating forest fires to smoke them out.
- Their numbers are reducing quickly.

Reading between the lines

Activity 2

Student 1 would achieve a lower grade and Student 2 a higher one.

Understanding structure and presentation

Activity 3

Presentational feature	Example	Effect of using it
Larger font	Heading and subheadings	Makes main ideas noticeable and draws reader's attention Emphasises key ideas or gives a summary of what a section is about
Text in panel	Heading on cover; heading on inside cover	Lifts writing off the page so it is more obvious for the reader
Bold	Every page in the subheadings and the main heading	Highlights key ideas Introduces what a certain part of the text is about
Bullet points	In the section 'Here are the shocking facts'	Abbreviates information Creates a quick list effect to make reading easier
Heading	Front cover and inside cover	Outlines the whole topic of the leaflet
Subheadings	Every page	Draws reader's focus in to key areas Summarises what each section is about
Logo	Front cover top left	Easily identifiable, in a prominent position, familiar to the reader
Colour	Every page	Makes leaflet more realistic Allows reader to see real image of the creatures

Practice 2

Bullet points are used as a presentational feature to involve the reader in the leaflet. This leaflet contains a lot of text that might be off-putting to some readers but the use of bullet points in the section 'Here are the shocking facts' means that information is made shorter and creates a quick list to make reading easier and quicker. Also, because this section is meant to shock and disturb the reader, the information needs to be snappy and concise to achieve this effect. It involves the reader and makes them want to read on and pick up vital facts and statistics promptly.

Green names the presentational feature

Pink explains how it appears in the leaflet

Yellow comments on how and why it involves the reader

Exploring persuasive language

Practice 3

Another example of emotive language used in the item is where the writer says 'A mother orang-utan never gives up her child without immense struggle ...'. These words are chosen as they make the reader see the effort that the mother will go to in order to protect her baby. For example, the phrase 'never gives up' makes us see that she will go to great lengths to save her child and suggests her determination in protecting what is hers. This is made clear by the use of the pronoun 'her' to show that it belongs to her and she will fight to save it. Moreover, the words 'immense struggle' imply that she will devote all her energy to protecting her child, and this makes us understand what she might have to go through one day. This has the effect of making us sympathise with her and want to help to prevent it from happening.

Pink selects an appropriate quotation

Blue analyses and comments on why the words are used

Yellow infers and interprets

Activity 4

Persuasive language technique	Example from text	Effect on reader
Emotive words – language that is used to appeal to the reader's emotions	never gives up her child without an **immense struggle**	Appeals to the reader's emotions by deliberately using words to affect their response – in this case to make us realise how much effort the mother will go to in order to protect her child
Directly talking to the reader – using words to make the reader feel that the writer is addressing them personally	With your help, WWF can continue to work	Draws the reader in and makes them feel like the text has been written for them
Statistics – numbers and percentages	but now less than **62,000** remain in the wild	Uses a number or percentage to show the facts and often to shock the reader
Superlatives – words showing something at its best or worst	orang-utan mothers are among **the most caring**	Shows something at its best
Directive – a gentle command or suggestion	Simply **complete the form** opposite	Gives an instruction or advice on what to do to help – sometimes a gentle nudge to support the charity
Rhetorical question – a question asked for effect where the answer is obvious	Will you help to protect them?	The answer is obvious after having read the whole text. The writer is assuming that the reader does not need to offer an answer

Practice 4

Emotive language to make the reader understand the plight of the orang-utans and to see how vital the WWF's work is

a 'nothing they can do to protect their babies from the threats of poaching'

b 'In the last 20 years Borneo has lost an area of orang-utan habitat 8 times the size of Wales'

Comparison – allows the reader to grasp just how much land is being destroyed

Use of personal pronoun to directly talk to the reader

c 'You don't need a stamp. But if you choose to use a stamp, even more of our precious funds'

Check your revision

Reading with understanding

- The ice is melting and this is ruining their habitat.
- There is illegal fishing going on in the area. This is taking their food.
- Climate change is affecting how they live.
- They live in one of the world's harshest environments.

Commenting on structure and presentation

Pictures are used in the web page to show the actual penguin in its natural habitat and better understand how and where it lives. The penguins are the focal point of the page and are easily noticed by the reader to interest them in their plight. One image is of a single penguin and the other one is of a small group of three. These are used to suggest that any donations made will help more than one penguin and allow groups to continue to live together.

Colours are used in the web page for various reasons. The text is white presented on a dark grey/black background. These contrasting colours make the writing stand out very well but also reflect the colours of the penguins. The colour red is used on a dark background to stand out but also to perhaps suggest the danger and threat that the penguins are under as red has connotations of danger and fear. Green is also used for some text to reflect the ideas about their natural environment that needs protecting.

Yellow infers and interprets

Blue refers to detail in the pictures

Pink considers the colours that are used

Thinking about language

Language to inform:

There is plenty of informative language in the web page to outline the situation of the penguins, highlight where they live and what they live on. Facts such as 'Adelie penguins nest and feed on the Antarctic sea ice'. This is not persuasive, simply factual and informative. Statistics are also used to convey information about penguins such as 'Approximately 2.5 million pairs in 160 colonies' to show the number of creatures that live there.

Language to persuade:

Coupled with the language to inform, the writer uses language to persuade because without this, the leaflet would just become a series of facts. These facts have to be blended with persuasive language if the web page is to be effective and encourage people to 'Adopt a Penguin'. This use of a gentle directive is prompting the reader to consider helping these creatures in a non-pressurised way. Similarly, the use of the personal pronoun 'you' is cleverly used to direct the text at the reader and make it feel more like a chat or informal discussion. This is meant to make the reader connect with the discussion more.

Green shows examples of language to inform

Blue shows examples of language to persuade

Pink shows examples from the text

Yellow shows how language has been used

Evaluating effectiveness

Effective:

The web page is effective in encouraging people to help penguins. The images are clear, and well placed to catch our attention and see what the natural habitat of the penguins is like and to show that it is worth preserving. Also the colours liven up the page with the clever use of red text to reflect the danger that the penguins are in and green text to imply that their homes need saving. The contrasting bold background and white text make it appear clear and inviting to read. The use of the word 'us' is effective in making us realise that the WWF have many people working on this campaign so it must be important and worth helping. Moreover, the use of different amounts of money to donate each month means that the reader feels less pressured into being told what to give — the choice is theirs.

Ineffective:

This web page is ineffective. It is structured in a similar way to many other persuasive texts with the use of a cute-looking creature in its own habitat to make us feel sorry for it. The pictures are meant to stand out and make us feel sorry for the penguins and they take up quite a bit of space on the page. This is done too often in persuasive texts so becomes overused. Similarly, the typical use of emotive language has little effect. Superlatives such as 'harshest' are predictable in creating a shocking environment in which to live in order to persuade the reader to donate money. Also phrases such as 'alarming rate' are simply someone's opinion — who is to say that it is 'alarming'?

Yellow says what you think

Pink shows examples to support points

Green explains why it is effective or not

Chapter 5: Exploring a personal recount

Reading for meaning

Activity 1
- Who – Stephen Evans.
- What – at the World Trade Center.
- Where – in New York.
- When – 11 September 2001.
- Why – to interview someone.

Activity 2
- The first jet went into the North Tower.
- He tried to persuade a newsagent to let him use his phone.
- The north tower collapsed.
- Cloud and debris came towards him.
- He ran ahead of the cloud of debris.

Practice 1

a *I only felt I was in danger once. When the North Tower collapsed, the whoosh of cloud and debris came towards me and I suddenly thought, 'That cloud's moving faster than I can run,' so I turned and fled, ahead of it.*

b

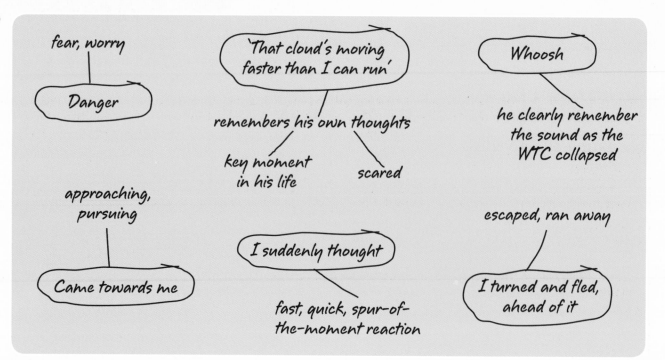

fear, worry

Danger

'That cloud's moving faster than I can run'

remembers his own thoughts

key moment in his life

scared

Whoosh

he clearly remember the sound as the WTC collapsed

approaching, pursuing

Came towards me

I suddenly thought

fast, quick, spur-of-the-moment reaction

escaped, ran away

I turned and fled, ahead of it

c and d

The writer reveals his fear in the language that he uses to describe and recount his experience. He uses the word 'danger' to imply that he was fearful and worried about the situation. He continues to reveal his fear when he describes the specific sound of the collapsing buildings by saying 'whoosh', which shows how noisy and frightening it must have been. Furthermore, when he says that the cloud of debris 'came towards me' it suggests that he is being pursued or followed and that he needs to escape. His fear develops when he says 'I suddenly thought', which shows that he has to act quickly and act on the spur of the moment. He even remembers his own thoughts as he quotes himself as this was probably a key moment in his life that he will never forget as it was so worrying. Finally, his fear is shown when he describes how he escaped from the situation by saying, 'I turned and fled, ahead of it'. So he ran away from what was frightening him.

Understanding structure and presentation

Activity 3

b He uses the present tense in the last paragraph.

Practice 2

The reader can tell that the writer 'can still feel the impact' by the detailed sentences that are used. For example, there are many clauses with noun phrases such as 'huge, solid door'. The adjectives 'huge' and 'solid' show just how powerful the impact was as both words suggest strength and size. Similarly, the writer uses active verbs such as 'slamming' and 'vibrating' as both show extreme force and energy and reinforce the impact in his writing.

Exploring the heading

Practice 3

The heading has been presented in a variety of ways to capture out attention. One way is by presenting it in bold text to outline the main idea of the text. Similarly, the writer uses contrasting words such as 'wrong' and 'right' to intrigue the reader and stimulate initial interest in the text. The words make the reader want to find out what it means by 'wrong' and 'right'. The heading is short and to the point so that it stands out and catches our attention.

Exploring language

Activity 5

Language technique	Example from the article	Comment on why it is used
Emotive language Words that appeal to our emotions or reveal feelings	devastation shudder ghastly	Emotive language is used to sway the reader to a certain point of view as the words chosen are meant to appeal to the emotions
Comparisons Comparing one thing or idea with another	It was like a huge, solid door slamming shut	Comparisons allow the reader to understand events or ideas that might never have happened to them so the comparison is usually something with which they can associate
Repetition A word or idea that is repeated over and over	whoosh	Repetition is used to stress a point or idea to the reader
Noun phrases An object or thing that has at least one or more adjective with it, e.g. compact, new car	most beautiful of New York mornings serene blue sky and the breeze of early autumn	Noun phrases give the reader a better picture of what is being discussed – the use of adjectives with the noun creates this

Evaluating effectiveness

Practice 5

The writer is effective in showing his feelings in the quotation. He uses language that makes the reader hear what is happening when he uses the word 'whoosh'. This example of onomatopoeia allows us to understand the 'impact' that he mentions as it suggests great energy and power. He goes on to add to his feelings by using a simile effectively to compare the impact so that the reader can understand how it felt 'like a huge solid door slamming shut'. He clearly remembers well how he felt as there is a lot of detail here in the noun phrase 'huge solid door'. Similarly, he uses the emotive word 'shudder' to show effectively how he felt scared and frightened at this point. It is clear that he tries to reflect his feelings in his choice of words.

Check your revision

Reading with understanding

- Hundreds of passengers were abandoned for hours beneath the Channel.
- Trapped in the darkness.
- On airless and stinking carriages.
- Thousands had Christmas ruined.

Commenting on structure and presentation

The headline is used for effect as it:

- rhymes with Eurostar (the train's name) and so creates humour
- the 'star' part of Eurostar is replaced with 'scarred' to imply that the company has developed a negative reputation
- it is short, to the point and stands out, so it will draw the reader in.

Thinking about language

Language is used in these ways by the writer to show disgust:

- Emotive words – 'failed' suggests poor service; 'abandoned' implies that they were just left with no help; 'trapped' shows that they were held captive in the train; 'airless' implies that they were probably uncomfortable as breathing would have been difficult; 'stinking' shows that it was unpleasant.
- Statistics – 'hundred' and 'five trains broke down' are used to show just how many people were affected and inconvenienced.
- The use of the word 'Incredibly' at the start of the sentence suggests that the writer is clearly astonished and shocked; similarly, the phrase 'on every level' implies that the company did nothing right to ease the situation or help customers.

Evaluating effectiveness

The writer is very effective in making his views clear about Eurostar:

- He uses emotive language to show that the company was incompetent in its dealings with the situation – words such as 'abandoned'; 'trapped'; 'stinking' all create a negative image of the situation.
- He uses a sarcastic pun in the headline 'Euroscarred' to show how the company will probably suffer in the future due to the situation.
- He uses statistics to show the sheer number of people who were inconvenienced by the situation 'hundreds'.
- He uses short and blunt simple sentences to make his opinions stand out and be very clear to the reader – 'The company failed its customers on every level'.

Chapter 6: More about comparison

Understanding the question

Practice 1

Look again at all three items. Each one has been <u>presented to entertain and interest</u> the reader.

Choose <u>two</u> of these Items. <u>Compare</u> them using these headings:

- the use of colour
- the pictures and diagrams.

You are now going <u>to compare two Items</u> out of the three you have read. They have all been <u>organised to interest and involve the reader</u>.

Choose <u>two</u> of these Items. <u>Compare</u> them using these headings:

- the headlines and subheadings
- the use of different fonts and bold text.

Understanding the examiner's mark scheme

Activity 2

- Focus more on the presentation.
- Show more detailed appreciation of the headings.
- More focus on the similarities and differences between the two items.

Check your revision

What is the question?

Look at how they are set out and organised

Look at the similarities and differences

Compare how headings are presented in both texts to interest the reader.

Make sure that you only write about two of them *not* three

Look at how they are set out and organised

Look at the similarities and differences

Compare the layout of both items.

Make sure that you only write about two of them *not* three

The words you need to remember

Words that show similarities	Words that show differences
Similarly	However
Also	In contrast
In addition	Alternatively
As well as	On the other hand
In the same way as	
Equally	

In Item 4.2 the heading is presented effectively as it says 'Euroscarred'. This is a sarcastic pun on the company name 'Eurostar' as the writer has changed 'star' to 'scarred' because he wants to criticize the company for its poor response to passengers trapped on Eurostar trains in the Channel Tunnel. In contrast, Item 5.2 uses the imperative 'Adopt a penguin' to gently suggest to the reader that this is what they should do. In addition, both headings are deliberately short to make the point clear and to involve the reader straight away. Similarly, both headings are in some ways emotive as the word 'adopt' suggests that penguins need help, and 'scarred' in 'Euroscarred' is a negative word aimed at the company and its reputation.

The skills you need to show

Purpose	Item 4.2 – web page	Item 5.2 – news report
To inform	Yes – plenty of factual information and images to outline the plight of penguins	Yes – plenty of detail outlining the events of the trains breaking down
To persuade	Yes – imperatives and emotive language suggest that the reader should respond by helping	Yes – biased text in which the writer condemns Eurostar for their poor response to stranded passengers
To explain	Yes – facts and figures given about the penguins	Yes – outlines the events of the situation
To instruct	Yes – use of imperatives to suggest that the reader gets involved with the WWF	No

Writing an answer

Compare the use of pictures in both items.

Item 5.2 is an opinion-based article from a newspaper so it is set out as you would expect this form to be. There are no pictures as the focus is mainly on the writer's opinion and we can assume that as the trains were stuck in dark tunnels beneath the sea, no photographs could have been taken. The writer uses short paragraphs to keep up the pace of the writing and to pack as much information into the piece as possible. Similarly, Item 4.2 is presented in short paragraphs to keep the reader interested and not overload them with too much information. However, Item 4.2 is much more visual in its layout as it is a persuasive text and needs to feature plenty of appropriate images. The penguins are presented in their natural habitat and are clearly positioned on the page to stand out to the reader. The background of the web page is deliberately black as it is bold and contrasts with white text – these are the same colours as the penguins to match the content. Green text is also used to suggest that the penguins need to be kept in their own environment. Furthermore, both items use short and snappy headings to capture the reader's attention and stress the topic of the whole text.

Yellow shows where the student has inferred and interpreted

Orange shows where the student has compared

Chapter 9: Answering the question

Planning

Practice 1

- Write a letter to the Chair of Governors at your school or college in which you argue that the school day should be shortened.
- Write the text for a leaflet advising parents on the most effective ways of dealing with their teenage children.
- Write the text for a speech persuading students at your school or college to support the charity of your choice.

Yellow is the subject

Pink is the purpose

Green is the audience

Blue is the form

Check your revision

- Twenty-five minutes.
- Plan.
- Five minutes.
- Read the question carefully; gather a range of ideas; decide on the order in which you will write about them; remind yourself of the skills you need to demonstrate in your writing; think of an engaging opening sentence.
- You need to be able to: engage and interest your audience; use Standard English; vary your sentence structures; make sure your meaning is clear; choose words for effect; make sure spelling and punctuation are accurate.
- Start thinking about how you are going to bring your writing to an end in the time you have left.

Chapter 10: Communicating clearly

Getting started

Activity 1

Student 1

After that, we could go shopping and buy loads and loads of exciting things to remind us of our stay at Blackpool or you could even win yourself some of the money you have spent in the arcades where there is a brill range of coin machines.

Student 2

If u was to come with me to Bangladesh u will see a place that is very special. I would just love it if u could live with my big, noisy extended family for a while whom I have left behind and come here to Britain which I like very much as well.

Student 3

We could visit Disneyland, Universal Studios, Big Bear town and Hollywood and having all these fab places around you will be awesome. The city of Los Angeles is great and is different to England where we go out shopping at 10am and finish at 5pm when everywhere shuts but people there and shops are open til about 11pm.

Activity 2

Student 1

After that, we could go shopping and buy many exciting things to remind us of our stay at Blackpool, or you could even win some money in the arcades where there is a brilliant range of coin machines.

Student 2

If you were to come with me to Bangladesh you would see a place that is very special. I would just love it if you could live with my big, noisy extended family for a while. I left them behind to come here to Britain, which I like very much as well.

Student 3

We could visit Disneyland, Universal Studios, Big Bear town and Hollywood and having all these fabulous places around you will be awesome. The city of Los Angeles is great and is different from England where we go out shopping at 10am and finish at 5pm when everywhere shuts. People there stay out late and the shops are open until about 11pm.

Check your revision

- Standard English.
- A rhetorical question; a series of short sentences; description.
- Link the ideas within each paragraph; make clear links between each paragraph and the one that follows it.

Chapter 11: Sentence structures and vocabulary

Sentence structures

Activity 1

- Complex
- Simple
- Compound
- Complex.

Activity 2

Simple sentences are used throughout **a**.

A mixture of simple, compound and complex sentences are used in **b**.

Practice 1

This is an example of a possible rewrite:

London, which is in the south-east of England, is the capital city. It has a population of about eight million people and is the world's ninth-largest city. London is on the banks of the River Thames and was the original settlement of the Romans. The City of London is known as the Square Mile. The Queen lives in Buckingham Palace in London.

Blue is a complex sentence

Green is a compound sentence

Yellow is a simple sentence

Changing word order

Activity 3

Here are some examples of different ways of writing the sentences:

- Having lost her doll in the park, the little girl cried all the way home.
- The little girl cried all the way home, having lost her doll in the park.
- Having met in an internet chat room, they married three years later.
- They married three years later, having met in an internet chat room.
- When the fire alarm rang, the sales assistant asked the customers to leave immediately.
- The sales assistant, when the fire alarm rang, asked the customers to leave immediately.

Vocabulary

Activity 4

Here is one way of rewriting the paragraph:

The very first thing we did was to go to their house and drop off our luggage. Then we set off to explore Greenwich. We stopped briefly at a café and had some lunch before going to the market. There was a huge range of things to see there, including some really good clothes stalls and a toy stall that fascinated my brother.

Sentence structure and vocabulary

Activity 5

First version	Improved version
The week was soon over	Sadly, the week was soon over
to go back	to return home
a really good holiday	a brilliant holiday
and our friends had enjoyed it too	and, fortunately, our friends had also enjoyed it
It was difficult to say goodbye	Saying goodbye was not easy
really good to	fantastic to
But we had to go	But we had to leave
another journey by boat	another scenic voyage
and then by tube	followed by the tube
and then by train from the station	and then, finally, the train from the same crowded station
when we got back	when we finally arrived

Check your revision

- A subject and a verb.
- A main clause makes complete sense on its own, a subordinate clause does not.
- A compound sentence has two or more main clauses which are joined by a conjunction such as 'and', 'so', 'or', 'but', 'because'.
- A complex sentence has at least one main clause and at least one subordinate clause.
- A range of simple, compound and complex sentences.
- In your exam you should aim to show the examiner that you have a wide vocabulary range. This means that you must choose the words you use carefully in order to have maximum impact on your reader.
- 'Tone' is the writer's attitude towards the subject and the reader. It can be serious, comic, sarcastic, formal, angry, friendly, and so on.

Chapter 12: Technical accuracy

Punctuation basics

Activity 1

The future holds many dreams and many worries for all of us. I don't know any student who knows what he or she wants to do on leaving school. Do you? There's a part of me which would just like to forget about getting qualifications and a job and travel the world. However, I know that if I did that, my mum would kill me and my Aunty Sarah would probably never talk to me again. Mr Sweeney, my ICT teacher, thinks I should try and get taken on by a large computer company such as IBM but I'd need good grades in my GCSEs so that I could go on and study further

Activity 2

Louise's best friend was planning to go into town on Saturday but Louise wasn't allowed to go with her. She'd asked her mother if she could, but was told she had to stay at home and look after her younger brother, Peter. Peter wasn't too happy about this either. If Louise was there, he wouldn't be able to go to the neighbour's house and play with Jason and, more importantly, Jason's new game.

Activity 3

- Kirsty and Adam were the most unlikely couple. They had met in Cranehill Secondary School and somehow managed to stay together when all their friends had gone in different directions. They had always known their lives would be spent with each other.
- This easy walk on the crags above Derwentwater in the Lake District is quite spectacular. Early September is the best time for the heather though the great wood, which is owned by the National Trust, is worth a visit at any time of year.
- 'Stop!' shouted the guard. 'If you go any further, we will shoot you.'
- It was his first day at school and he needed to think carefully about what he should take: the shiny lizard pencil case, his best Batman cape, an apple and his brand-new laser fighter.
- 'Haven't you got any more money?' he asked in despair.

Punctuation: advanced

Activity 4

i The fridge contained half a pint of sour milk, a lump of mouldy cheese, a half-eaten trifle and a tired-looking lettuce.

ii Imran Qureshi, aged 42 and father of three, was the first to arrive at the crime scene.

iii Having closed the door firmly behind her, Mrs Bright forgot to turn the key.

iv He leapt out of his seat as soon as his mother called, 'Dinner's ready!'

Spelling: basic rules

Activity 5

Here are some examples of words you could have formed:

Agree: agreeable; disagree; agreement; disagreed.

Inform: misinform; informing; informed.

Fair: unfair; fairly.

View: review; viewed; viewable; viewing.

Reverse: irreversible; reversing; reversed.

Believe: believable; unbelievable; believing; disbelieving; believed.

Perfect: perfection; imperfect; perfectly; perfected.

Success: successful; unsuccessful; successfully.

Activity 6

lunches Mondays Christmases beaches radiuses/radii ladies atlases inches women blushes comedies cactuses/cacti takeaways hoaxes stitches ferries bonuses pluses essays gases arches coaches keys wishes blotches bullies doormen hippopotamuses/hippopotami mediums/media scissors

Activity 7

a We're going into town where we are hoping to find something new to wear to the wedding.

b The prophet said he would bring peace to the land.

c The whole of the great hall, including the ceiling, was bathed in sunshine.

d They're not allowed to go in there until their muddy boots are removed.

Check your revision

- Inverted commas are used:
  - when a writer uses a speaker's actual words, for example: 'I'm sorry,' said the receptionist, 'but the doctor is busy.'
  - when a writer is quoting from another text, for example: Larkin wrote this poem for a new-born girl who he refers to as a 'tightly-folded bud'.
- Won't; shan't.
- The correct use of commas within a sentence is often an indicator of a more able student.
- Breaking a word into syllables and sounding each syllable aloud can remind you of letters you may have missed out.
- A prefix is a group of letters that can be added to the beginning of a root word to change its meaning. A suffix is a letter or group of letters that can be added to the end of a root word to change its meaning.
- Sheep, crises, tomatoes, roofs, taxis, flies.

Chapter 13: Targeting your audience

Engaging the reader

Activity 3

> 12 Carney Close
> Leelham
> Bandford
> BA24 9SG
>
> 10/06/2010
>
> Dear Mr Cooper,
>
> My child Tracey Sleetham has been a pupil at your school for 3 years now. I am extremely happy with her grades, the teachers and everything else in general. However, I am highly appauled at the amount of physical activity they get a week. One hour! No wonder child obesity is a huge issue these days. What do they expect? Luckily I encourage my child to do all of school clubs.
>
> I feel every child would benefit a great deal from putting just one hour a day of activities in place. Firstly, it would help a lot of children who have weight issues to bring there confidence back. Do you feel it's really fair to take away a childs confidence? They are 5–10 years old! They don't know how to look after themselves. That is why they need us. Secondly, it would be a great way for the children to socialise with others and make new friends from other classes. Lastly, it would be a genius way of granting the children a fun reward for excelent behaviour, persuading children to be well behaved throughout the day.
>
> I've thought through my argument very considerably and understand there will be a few minor obstacles which will occur. For example: how will you find this time? Well, there are four one hour and fifteen minute lessons throughout the day. You could cut the lessons by one fifth which will equal out an hour which you could use for this.
>
> Thank you for your time and I am looking forward to speaking to you very soon.
>
> Yours sincerely
> Linda Sleetham

Annotations:
- Addresses the headteacher by name
- Explains her connection with the school
- Says positive things about the school
- Uses a rhetorical question to encourage the headteacher to think about the issue
- Uses a first-person plural pronoun to put herself and the headteacher on the same side
- Shows that there are benefits for the headteacher
- Shows she has considered the issue from the headteacher's point of view
- Thanks the headteacher for reading the letter
- Shows that she hopes to speak with the headteacher later